2nd Edition

Broken Beyond Belief has been translated into Russian & Spanish.

Broken Beyond Belief

BROKEN BEYOND BELIEF

BY VIDA BUCKLEY

Broken Beyond Belief

Copyright © 2017 Vida Buckley. All rights reserved.

Published by

DHANI Publishing Company

www.incrediblesupport8ministries.com

Graphic Design Chris Middleton

Artist and Illustrator: Aaron A. Hicks

All rights reserved. This book or parts thereof may not be reproduced in any form, stored in a retrieval system, or transmitted in any form by an means - electronic, mechanical, photocopy, recording, or otherwise - without prior written permission of the author, except as provided by United States of America copyright law.

Unless otherwise identified, scripture quotations are from the Holy Bible King James Version, Cambridge, 1769. Used by permission. All rights reserved.

Any name referencing satan will not be given the respect of capitalization, even at the risk of improper sentence structure.

ISBN-13: 978-0-692-97178-9

Library of Congress Control Number: 2017916815

Printed in the United States of America.

DEDICATION

In loving memory of my parents.

Because they once lived, I now live and can tell my story.

My mommy instilled inside of me, my basic Christian principles.

My daddy instilled discipline in me, for he was a workaholic and an awesome provider.

I love you both with all of my heart!

ACKNOWLEDGEMENTS

Thanks to my family and friends who have touched my life in a positive way.

I would like to thank my daddy and my mommy; although, they've made their transitions to be with the Lord, they're here in spirit with me.

I would like to give special thanks to my godmother, Tinietta Ellis, one of my biggest fans and supporters.

Special thanks go to my brother Lee Henry Lewis, my sister Zina Bey-Rush and my niece Valerie Latham, who at some point in time gave me some good advice and direction along the way.

I would like to give a very special thanks to my son, Donnie Smith, who constantly helps me to stay encouraged and motivated.

I would like to give thanks to my husband, Gerald Buckley who at the start of my writing journey with this book was my fiancé.

Last but not least, I give thanks to God All Mighty who continually shows me that I can do all things through Christ Jesus!

PREFACE

I believe that we all have a story to tell from our life experiences.

    Actors try to act it out...

        Preachers try to preach it out...

            Rappers try to rap it out...

                Singers try to sing it out...

It's all about what inspired you to tell your story and generally, in most cases, your story comes from past pain, past hurts, past life experiences but somehow you survived what was intended to destroy you. Not only did you survive but you survived to tell a story, your story; a story that would help and encourage those who think that they are at the end of their road. Perhaps you are not at the end of your road but at a crossroad and you just need to make a real, life-changing decision.

So often when people come to a crossroad, they think that they are at the end of their dead-end road; this makes the person feel hopeless and helpless at times because they think that they are stuck in a situation instead of having a solution for the situation.

If you have more problems than solutions, or if you have more excuses than solutions, then this book is for you. Even if you were at a dead end, couldn't you just make a U-turn? In real life when you are driving in your vehicle and you might go the wrong way or get lost and find yourself at a dead-end road, what is the normal thing to do? You put your car in reverse and you turn around. So often in life if we would just make a U-turn in some of our situations, the outcome would have been much better; all I'm saying is that everything bad that happens in our lives isn't necessarily the end. Sometimes we just need to change directions to get back on course.

Have you noticed that life's lessons tend to take us on a journey? Well relax and enjoy the journey, even when the adventurous journey has some twists and turns. We learn from our lessons in life. These experiences, in turn, become some of our best teachers. Never regret being who you are because of the choices that you've made; only learn from them and become a better you and move on to bigger and better things.

I invite you to come and follow me as I share the joys and jeers of my journey.

John 10:10 – the thief cometh not, but for to steal, and to kill, and to destroy: I am come that they might have life, and that they might have it more abundantly.

Table of Contents

DEDICATION 6

ACKNOWLEDGEMENTS 6

PREFACE 8

FOREWORD 12

LIFE'S JOURNEY 14

NOW AND LATER 86

WHO DID IT? AND HOW DID IT HAPPEN? 120

COPING WITH LOSS 132

COPING WITH BROKEN PROMISES 154

IF SEASONS CHANGE - WHY NOT YOU? 177

YOU'VE GOT TO MOVE FOR THE BLESSING 183

THE ELEVENTH HOUR 188

A BROKEN ECONOMY BEING MADE WHOLE ... 192

ABOUT THE AUTHOR 208

FOREWORD

I feel truly blessed and honored to tell you about this *"Virtuous and God-Fearing Woman,"* Evangelist Vida Buckley.

I have known Evangelist Buckley for over twenty-nine years and I know it was no coincidence in how we met. I had just started a new job and met Evangelist Buckley in the cafeteria where we both worked. She and a few other women were sitting at a table opposite me, and I did not know many people at the company since I had just recently started. I sensed in my spirit that there was something different about the women at the table. So, as I proceeded to leave the cafeteria, I stopped by the table Evangelist Buckley was sitting and said hello and asked if they were Christians. We all smiled at the same time and they invited me to sit with them and we had a short meet and greet. And yes, they were Christians and women who were sold out for Christ. They felt just as I did . . . *that this meeting was God appointed.*

Since that day in 1990, Evangelist Buckley and I have become the best of friends/sisters (*since I never had a sister*). Evangelist Buckley has been just like a sister to me through the good times and the trials. She is definitely a true friend who is there for me during the times I have needed her. She loves the Lord with all her heart, soul, and mind and does not waver in her faith.

Evangelist Buckley preaches and teaches the unadulterated word of God and speaks what He has her to speak to His people. She has a compassion for the broken-hearted, abused, lonely, and lost souls. She and her husband, Elder Gerald Buckley, is an excellent example of how a marriage should be as God would have us to love, give, and cherish one another.

I know this book will bless, encourage, and uplift your spirit. Her story is about things she has experienced during her life. In each chapter, she shares the trials and triumphs she has gone through and how you can overcome and conquer your trials with the help of our Lord and Savior Jesus Christ.

Prophetess Sherwin Gaston

LIFE'S JOURNEY

What inspired me to write this book is something that came from deep within, a hurt that reached deep down to the core of my existence, a hurt that is, at times, difficult to explain. It happened during the end of my second marriage, where it involved three small children whom I grew to love dearly and suddenly all in one day the marriage and children were all taken away from me.

Yes, I'm the one who had to leave the marriage but the choice was not mine. When a marriage ends in divorce and there are children involved, the husband and the wife are not the only ones who are affected by the divorce. The children are just as devastated as the parents or parent.

There were two parents in the home, now there is only one parent. The home has become broken and the children, in their own way, have their brokenness too. They have their thoughts about the situation too. What happened? I thought they loved each other. Sure parents have arguments and disagreements, but wasn't the love supposed to make everything alright? Not only are the children broken, they're probably confused too.

There was no explanation other than my then husband said that our relationship was not working for him and that it was too much work for him; it was too hard. I did ask how it was too hard but I got no answer. Of course, I don't have to tell you that I was messed up, devastated, bamboozled, hoodwinked, and led astray! Simply put, I was deeply hurt.

What is hurt? Webster Dictionary states that hurt is an emotional pain or anguish that can cause harm, distress, pain, injury, wounds, and damage. When a person is hurt, it is an indication that some event in their life has caused a form of wound and damage. We can look at hurt as being similar to an open wound; when you have hurt that has not been healed, anytime someone rubs you the wrong way or rubs up against that wound, you still can feel the pain. The Holy Bible speaks of hurt as a broken spirit and a broken heart.

> ***Psalm 51:17*** *– The sacrifices of God are a broken spirit: a broken and a contrite heart, O God, thou wilt not despise.*

Therefore, we know that when healing takes place, not only is my heart but also my inner man (which is my spirit) is being mended. Anything that is broken needs to be fixed, put back together, and made whole. John stated *beloved above all things I wished that you would prosper and be in health but as your soul prospers* (3 John 2 Paraphrase). This lets us know that the healing must begin on the inside first and then reach to the outside.

When you have been broken, accept that you will experience some pain. Do NOT try to suppress your feelings. Although it would be easy to say bad or negative things, do NOT slander the person. When you lose something or someone important to you, always remember that feeling sad is a natural emotion. Do NOT and I repeat do NOT continue to replay the bad memories. Replaying bad memories will get you stuck in your emotions. Feeling angry, hurt and/or sad will only lead to you being depressed and in distressed.

When you are grieving, remember your family and friends would love to support you and have the right words to say. In most cases, when you're hurting there are not many words that will help the pain go away. It's at these times that you must hold on to your faith and go through the process so that you can grow through the process.

Have you ever been hurt so deeply that you felt like you could NOT breathe? This is the body's way of coping with the pain, but begin to breathe; even if they're small breaths, breathe slowly and think about the goodness of the LORD anyhow.

Always remember the ending of something generally is the beginning of something new. **DO** nice things for yourself, **DO NOT** be afraid to spend some alone time with yourself. **DO NOT** be afraid to treat yourself to a dinner or a movie but most importantly **DO** spend some alone time with your Heavenly Father. Meditate on the word...*I can **DO** all things through Christ which strengthens me* (Philippines 4:13). Tell yourself over and over I CAN DO THIS! I can **DO** all things and yes, you can get over this too. This too shall pass!

While you're forgetting the old (bad) memories, start remembering the great qualities about yourself, like you are fearfully and wonderfully made, that God knew you before He formed you in your mother's womb and that God has great plans for your life. This is not the end but in fact a new beginning for you. Isn't it funny how sometimes-in life before one door can open another door must close?

American writer Barbara Bloom once noted, "When the Japanese mend broken objects, they aggrandize the damage by filling the cracks with gold. They believe that when something's suffered damage and has a history, it becomes even more beautiful." What a beautiful analogy for what God does with our brokenness! Bring all your cares and worries to the One who has the power to heal your broken heart.

Let's fill up our cracks with so much love, joy, and happiness. So much, in fact until your brokenness becomes something to share. Fill it until you can find the goodness in your brokenness; fill it until it no longer hurts. That's when you will be able to help someone else.

In some, certainly not all cases, when a relationship or marriage ends; there could be a level of abuse that happens in the relationship that we do not understand or even recognize. Even if you recognize the abuse, sometimes a person will not want to talk about it because of the embarrassment or fear of what others might have to say. How did you let this happen? Why did you put up with the abuse? Why didn't you tell me or someone in authority? You can also be in an emotionally or mentally abusive relationship and not realize it. Even in my marriage that ended in divorce, I did not know that I had experienced mental abuse until the judge stated that my divorce was being granted because of mental abuse.

Sometimes you can go through or be involved in abusive situations and not know that you are being abused until somebody puts a label on it. Generally, it takes someone from the outside looking in to make such an observation, especially if you are not being physically hit or harmed.

Hurt can come at the hands of many things, but by far one of the worst forms of hurt results from abuse. We see and hear about a lot of abuse in our society today, whether the abuse is physical, mental or emotional. Sometimes when a person has been physically abused, we tend to see the scars left behind after the abuse. From my personal experience, I discovered that emotional and mental abuse can be just as bad as physical abuse.

With emotional abuse, you know that the hurt is there because you still feel pain that you tried to bury deep within your soul. With mental abuse, you know the hurt is there because as much as you try to forget, the abuse and the abuser is always on your mind tormenting you. Some people do not know how to escape the thoughts from the abuse because the pain runs so deep that you see no way around it, under it, over it, or through it. Although there may be no outward evidence or visible scarring, emotional and mental abuse leaves your spirit and soul with scars that need to be healed.

Scars are not all bad because a scar generally forms only after a wound has healed. Although, a scar means that a form of healing is in process, I also recognize that we must properly heal if we want to be made whole. I've noticed in the Bible whenever Jesus healed someone, He always asked the person if they wanted to be made whole; I've never read where Jesus asked the person if they wanted to be made half. When we're made whole, then that means we will be healed completely in spite of what transpired in the past.

According to the Strong's Concordance, **whole** is derived from the Greek word **ischuō**, *is-khoó-o*, which means to have (or exercise) force (lit. or fig.), to be able, avail, can do, could be good, might, prevail.

Allow your faith to help make you whole like the woman with the issue of blood. She had heard so many great things about Jesus that she said to herself, *if she could just touch the hem of Jesus' garment, she knew that she would be made whole* (Matthew 9:21). There's one little problem... the Book of Leviticus (Chapter 15) lets us know if a woman had an issue of blood, for as long as she had the issue, she was not to be out in the public around people. If she did, she could risk losing her life because the law carried a death sentence for anyone who would dare to break such a law.

The woman with the issue not only pressed past the law, but she pressed past the crowd and she pressed into Jesus to touch the hem of His garment. The moment she touched Jesus' garment, not only did she touch Jesus with her hand, but she touched Jesus with her faith. When she touched Jesus with her faith, it was at that moment she was made whole; it was at that moment she was able to prevail. Prevail against what? She was able to prevail against the illness that had her bound for 12 long years, she was able to prevail past what would have ordinarily been an obstacle (the crowd) and prevail against the law. Under the Mosaic Law, a woman with an issue of blood (referring to menstrual or postpartum bleeding) was considered unclean and was "put apart" for 7 days (Leviticus 15). During this time, anything she lay on or sat on was considered "unclean," meaning that if anyone touched one of those things, he would have to wash his clothes and bathe in water to become clean again.

The Mosaic Law also specified that if a woman had an issue of blood that lasted longer than 7 days that all the days of her issue were considered unclean and she must be treated as such (Leviticus 15: 25). This means that this woman had probably been unclean for 12 years and that she had to live separated and/or alone from others for that period of 12 years. Can you imagine being isolated from everyone and everything for 12 years? I know I enjoy my alone time, but **12 LONG YEARS**? If she had been married, her husband probably would have divorced her, as she would have been unable to care for her children or for others without making them all unclean. Her unclean status would also have meant that she was unable to attend the temple or other worship services. I could ONLY imagine the isolation and rejection she must have felt. I wonder if she felt abandoned by God.

This woman with the issue of blood was able to press past all of the obstacles (crowd, Jewish laws, sickness, etc.) and touch Jesus in such a way that the healing power would be released from Jesus. Yes, the woman with the issue of blood allowed her faith to release her healing. Although the woman with the issue of blood had a different issue, she still had an issue where she needed to be healed and so does the person that has been broken; yes, you need to be made whole too.

I was involved in a terrible car accident in August 2009 where I had gotten seriously injured. I was at the corner and I was about to turn into the complex of where I lived at the time. What was so strange about this entire car accident is that I had just driven all the way from Joliet, Illinois without any incidents or accidents. It was a seven-car lane: three car lanes going south and four-car lanes coming north.

I was facing south where the four-car lanes were. As I was waiting to make my turn, I watched the traffic lights turn from green to yellow. I remembered waiting and thinking that these cars are not stopping so I waited until all the three lanes of cars came to a complete stop; the light has now turned to red. I'm thinking surely, it's safe to turn now but something happened; a young woman ran a red light and crashed into the passenger side of my car.

As my car began to spin, I knew that I was in the midst of a car accident that was going to be very bad. Somehow, while my car was still spinning, our cars met up again and the back of our cars hit; this second hit made us go into another spin. I could see a bright light so white I can only try to describe the white as a pure white that I had never seen before. It was at that moment a total peace came over me and I knew that everything would be okay. I have to be honest in confessing that I do believe that 'pure white' that I was seeing inside my vehicle was an Angel. I believe this for a few reasons: I never saw a pure white like that, I had a peace during the entire car accident, and I had a knowing that no matter how bad this accident would be that I would be okay.

As I looked to my right, I could see the passenger air bag deploying. The air bag looked like an off-white color, almost like a crème or beige color up against the bright white that I was seeing inside of my vehicle therefore, it was at that moment that I turned my head because I knew that the driver's side, my air bag would soon deploy as well and it did. I only got a slight a bruise on my jaw from my (the driver's) air bag. I told myself as soon as the car stop spinning, to hurry up and get out of the vehicle. As soon as the car stopped spinning, I unlocked my seat belt and I pushed the door open.

I remembered the door being heavy to push because the impact of the accident had somehow disfigured the driver's door as well. When I stepped out of the vehicle, I was dizzy from the car spinning. I could remember the weather that day… the sun was shining bright; it was very nice and clear. I also remember there being a nice amount of people on the sidewalk. You could see the amazement on their faces and you could feel the excitement in the air. An older man came to assist me but I could also see the astonishment in his eyes. He told me that he wanted to help me and to see if I was okay. I told the older man that I thought that I was okay. Then he said, "no you're not, look down at your leg; it's bleeding."

Once I knew that I was hurt, I grabbed the man's arm and kind of limped to the sidewalk. When I got to the sidewalk, there was a police officer on the scene and he told me to sit down on the sidewalk because I was hurt. The witnesses began to tell me that the young lady was coming fast and that she had ran the red light. While I set on the curb listening to the different voices, I looked in the middle of the street to see my car, mangled and pointed west. I then asked the officer, "where is the other car that was involved in the accident?" He pointed behind me. The car had gone past all of the bystanders, the sidewalk, some trees and a steel box and ended up on the grass in front of a tree. Wow! I then asked the officer where is the other person or persons that was involved in the accident? The officer pointed to the ground. The young lady was in her vehicle by herself, just as I was, and there she laid on the ground unconscious.

It was at that point my heart began to race, my thoughts became cloudy, and I began to ask the officer hysterically is the young lady okay? After the officer said that she was unconscious, he would not say anything else. When the paramedics arrived, I asked them to go over to see if the young woman was okay? I'm now praying down Heaven, calling on Jesus, asking Him to allow the young woman to live and not die. At this point, you do not care who is at fault; you just do not want to be involved in accident where someone is seriously hurt. So I kept asking my paramedics to go see about the young lady but the paramedic explained that they were assigned to me and that her paramedics is assigned to her and that they could not leave me and that her paramedics could not leave her.

The paramedics began to explain that they are going to lift the young lady onto the stretcher first and that her ambulance is going to take off first due to her being unconscious and then they were going to lift me onto my stretcher and take off right after her. I had no problem with that all. One thing that the officer said to me that sticks in my mind is that he had assessed the damage and that both vehicles were totaled on the spot and that he had seen accidents with less damage to the cars and the people had more severe bodily injuries than what the young lady or myself had endured.

I remember arriving at the hospital and hearing them call code blue. The paramedics had taken us to the same hospital. The officer came to the hospital; he told me that the lady was in the room next to mine and he told me that the lady had regained consciousness but that the hospital was going to keep her overnight for observation just as a precautionary measure. Praise the Lord for answered prayers! Halleluiah!

I do thank God that there were no fatalities and everyone involved was okay, meaning neither she nor I sustained any life-threatening injuries. I had to a have a bone replacement surgery for my leg. My doctor appeared to be more concerned about the therapy after the surgery. My doctor said, "If you don't have the proper therapy in place before the surgery, then I will not perform the surgery. Without proper therapy (proper healing), you would be handicapped for the rest your life." He did not reveal the level and severity of the handicap but I guess I would have walked with a limp or something.

This made me think about being properly healed in every area of our lives, whether it would be physically, mentally, spiritually or emotionally. Many people are wise enough to frequent the psychiatrist when they have situations that are mentally disturbing to them. They have moved beyond the point of caring about others' opinions and their potential to be made fun of; they know that the psychiatrist is mental therapy that can help them process emotional pain. Allowing the therapist to help them to become, or to remain functional, rather than allowing that devastating situation(s) that deeply wounded them, to overtake them. The emotional pain could have messed them up for life if they would have allowed themselves to get stuck in the pain, get stuck in the turmoil, and not have been able to move forward. Just as we need physical therapy to heal properly on the outside we need inner healing for our entire being in order to heal properly.

> ***Luke 4:18-19 –*** *[18] The Spirit of the Lord is upon me, because he hath anointed me to preach the gospel to the poor; he hath sent me to heal the brokenhearted, to preach*

deliverance to the captives, and recovering of sight to the blind, to set at liberty them that are bruised, [19] To preach the acceptable year of the Lord.

I believe that we all need therapy (cure, help, rehabilitation, remedy, and treatment) at some point and time in our life to keep us from becoming paralyzed (stuck) or handicapped; we need to be delivered. We need this help, not just in our physical beings but in every area of our lives, our mind, our soul, and our spirit. Yes, I believe that therapy can help you but even more that, I believe God is the only One that can totally make you whole you and heal the deep wounds. The wounds that go so deep that it touches your soul…the wounds that you do not know how to describe, nor care to share with many people. You can't see the wounds with your naked eye but you know that they are there. Yes, those wounds.

When God is able to heal you and make you whole that is called deliverance. What Jesus said in Luke 4 was a direct quote from Isaiah 61:1,2 when He said, "the Spirit of the Lord is upon me…" Jesus let us know exactly what He had come to this earth to do and that was to deliver all His people, no matter who you are and what is holding you captive; He clearly let us know His mission and His objective. Jesus' ministry was about deliverance; He came here on a rescue mission. If you have ever been in bondage, if you have ever been in chains or locked up for any reason and a person was sent to deliver you, to set you free, to rescue you, there is an eternal appreciation to this person for coming to rescue you. Yes, Jesus is that Person and He came to set us free.

Even in our churches today, we see very little deliverance-taking place. Are we afraid to pray for others? Are we afraid to receive prayer? Are we afraid that the preacher is going to tell us where we've been and where we're going? What we're doing and what we're not doing? Always remember that God is the author and finisher of our faith. God knows where we started out and God knows the plans that He has for our lives. Trust me, God's plan for your life is that we will excel, that we will exceed and that we will expand! How do I know this? Because Jesus said that *He came that we might have life and that more abundantly* (John 10:10). Do you want everything that God has for you?

Broken Beyond Belief

When we look at a person, it doesn't matter the level of success that one has accomplished in their career or life. A person who has been traumatized in their early childhood and never received the counseling, the deliverance, the help that they needed, their facial expressions change, their body language tends to change and you can see the hurt forming and the tears wailing up in their eyes whenever they began to talk about that 'thing' that happened when they were three, four or five, etc. years of age; this is when we must realize that they have not had the proper therapy or healing to process what has happened to them. Most of times, we want the person to forget about what has happened and focus on the rest of their lives but they are stuck in that area of their life until they get the proper healing or therapy they need to move past that painful ordeal(s). Some people go on to achieve great success but still need to be healed and made completely whole. Just telling a person they need to get over it does not empower them to make it happen immediately; it just means that they will hide their hurt around you or avoid you. You cannot compare your story to their story but you can always pray for their healing and wholeness.

We have heard the overly stated cliché, "hurting people hurt people." It's stated so much for a reason. When a person has been deeply hurt and they have not properly healed, that hurting person will at some point in time, lash out at other people and hurt them as well in the form of a verbal or physical confrontation. Sometimes this is done maliciously and at other times it happens "unexplainably" and unplanned. Think about it – when you are hurt, hurt can sometimes bring about anger and anger mixed with hurt that has not been dealt with cooks up bitterness. So, the hurt person that did not heal properly is walking around with unidentified and/or unaddressed bitterness.

Many times we look at this type of person as not taking any mess from anyone or even being hostile, when really they are just hurting deep down inside and just screaming silently within "I don't know what to do but I need to be made whole."

Needing to be made whole could stem from a childhood memory of something that happened to you when you were a child; if you didn't heal properly then you are not the whole person that you need to be or that God intended for you to be.

The first time I could remember being emotionally and mentally distressed was when I was around four years of age and my step grandfather, Poppa Seal passed away on Christmas Eve. I was confused, being that I wasn't at all familiar with death but I felt the sadness throughout our entire household. I could see the sadness all over my mother's face and pain was in her eyes.

I didn't know it at that time but hurt would be a companion of mine throughout this journey called life. Although I have been intimately acquainted with hurt, I cannot say that hurt has been a constant companion of mine. Even when I do experience hurt, I can vouch that joy has also been present.

The joy that comes from the Lord does not disappear because life happens or your other emotions of sadness, hurt and/or anger are prevalent and present. If this would be the case, then that would mean that God's joy is temporary and is ONLY based on good circumstances. God and the Word of the Lord should be the greatest source of joy no matter what is or appears to be going on in our lives. Yes, it's easy to be happy when everything is going well, it's easy to be happy because of winning the lottery, it's easy to be happy when you get a promotion on your job. However, the joy of the Lord is something that only those who truly trust and believe in the Lord can have in spite of any circumstance.

John 15:11 where Jesus says, *"These things I have spoken to you, that my joy may be in you, and that your joy may be full."* The reason this text is so important is that Jesus refers to His own joy as being in us — not just Him giving us joy, but Jesus joy dwelling on the inside of us. We are not just rejoicing over what we know about Jesus, we are rejoicing with the very joy of Jesus over what He knows about everything, especially what He knows about our Father in Heaven.

The joy of the Lord comes from properly understanding God's Word.

> **John 15:11** – *"These things I have spoken to you, that my joy may be in you, and that your joy may be full."*

When we are cognizant of the fact that God, in His Divine Power, has already given us everything we need in this life, no matter what the situation might be, we will be able to celebrate in the good news of not having to face any of these situations alone.

What we have already learned and know about the Lord and surrounding ourselves with the things of God can bring you joy and can help you to overcome any situation, even the bad ones...especially the bad ones. There are far too many things to do rather than lay or sit there doing nothing, wallowing in your hurt and misery. Read the Bible; pray meditate on the Word of God. Go to a musical, a gospel concert, an extra church service, etc. We should be able to find joy in the fact of knowing we belong to God and that God belongs to us. Our joy does not exist because of perfect situations but our joy exists because of us being in a Perfect Christ.

> ***1 Thessalonians 1:6** (NIV) – You became imitators of us and of the Lord, for you welcomed the message in the*

midst of severe suffering with the joy given by the Holy Spirit.

The Thessalonians endured hard trials and persecutions but just as the Apostle Paul wrote a letter to encourage the church at Thessalonica for receiving the message of Salvation with joy, you too must be encouraged through your hard trials and know that your joy is forever within you. It's at times like these that you have to allow your faith to connect with your joy.

***1 Peter 1:8-9** (NIV) – Though you have not seen Him (Jesus), you love Him; and even though you do not see Him now, you believe in Him and are filled with an inexpressible and glorious joy, 9 for you are receiving the end result of your faith, the salvation of your souls.*

Weeping may endure for a night but joy comes in the morning (Psalm 30:5). This lets you know that God recognizes that we will have some experiences here in the earth that will bring tears to our eyes but even in our darkest hour, we must always remember that morning is coming. When the morning time comes in our circumstances, this will be a time of refreshing and rejoicing.

Nehemiah 8:10 – *for the joy of the LORD is your strength!*

I often looked at that scripture in two ways:

1) If I do the things that please the LORD, not only would I have joy but He would give me strength too.
2) Because of the joy that I have in the LORD, I also have strength.

You never know how strong you are, until being strong is your only choice~~Bob Marley

Why do we need strength? We need strength to move on. As Bob Marley so aptly put it, "you don't know how strong you are until being strong is the only choice you have. It's hard to move on if you don't let go. Exercising on a regular basis is what helps a person to become strong. Exercising (training) our minds will help us to become mentally and emotionally stronger. How does one train their mind? It's what we allow to come into our thought patterns. If it's not of God, 2 Corinthians 2:5 says to *cast down every thought that exalt itself against the knowledge of God....* If it's not of God, then it is not something you should be thinking on. It's important to take control of our thoughts or our thoughts will take control of us. How we take hold of our thoughts, is by meditating on goodness of the Lord.

> ***Philippians 4:8*** *– Finally, brethren, whatsoever things are true, whatsoever things are honest, whatsoever things are just, whatsoever things are pure, whatsoever things are lovely, whatsoever things are of good report; if there be any virtue, and if there be any praise, think on these things.*

By meditating and reading the above scripture out loud, you can begin to renew your thought pattern; you can begin to renew your mind. When our minds are being renewed, our thought patterns are changing and we are being transformed. When we are being transformed, our character is making a radical change.

> **Romans 12:2** – *"Be ye transformed by the renewing of your mind, that ye may prove what is that good, and acceptable, and perfect, will of God"*

You may ask, "How do I surround myself with the things of the LORD?" Well, many Christian people may know how to do this but what if you don't know or what if you are not a Christian? The first step would be to accept Jesus into your heart. It's as simple as confessing this prayer. Repeat after me:

> *Lord Jesus, I ask You to come into my heart. I acknowledge that I am a sinner. Forgive me of all my sins.*

I believe and confess that you are the Son of God who died and was raised. Be Lord of my life for the rest of my life. In Your Name, amen.

Welcome to the family of God! You have made the best decision of your life. To help you learn and grow in this new life as a Christian (or if you've been saved any length of time), I would work on doing the following:

1) If you don't own a Bible, then you should purchase a Bible. There are many types of Bibles but you can decide which version is best for you. For new believers or for those who are seeking a more simplistic translation, I suggest the New King James Version.

2) Make sure that you set time aside each day to read your Bible. If you miss a day or two, please do not beat up on yourself.

3) Find a church that you can feel comfortable in and that teaches truths from the Bible. If the church does not teach that Jesus is the Messiah and He is the ONLY

way, then they are not teaching from a true biblical perspective.

4) One of the best ways I've learned and grown over the years is by attending Bible Study and Sunday School. These are more intimate times of teaching and sharing that allows you to ask questions about the Bible and how to live life as a Believer.

5) Pray that God will send you a trustworthy prayer partner to help encourage you and to strengthen you. This will help build you up in your holy faith.

After you have taken the above steps, I promise you will not only form a personal relationship with God but you will learn so much about Him and it will enable you to learn so much more about yourself as well. Have you ever asked yourself, "Why do I keep going through the same things? If you have changed the course of your action and you are still producing the same results, then you have to know that something outside of the natural realm is affecting you and the things that you do. This is called the spiritual realm. A lot of people do not like to talk about the spiritual realm because the unknown at times can be a bit scary and confusing. I have to admit that I'm not comfortable with everything that I know about the spiritual realm but I believe if we live in the natural realm, we must be willing to understand some things about the spiritual realm if we want to be successful in getting past our present situation(s), especially if our current situation has held us captive or in some type of bondage.

Whether we recognize it or not, there's a battle going on inside of us. We can feel the struggle inside and around us. Sometimes we can feel or sense other people's spirit or personal battles that they are currently facing.

Sometimes the battle that we are in is not visible to the naked eye and sometimes you or someone that you know might have difficulty trying to explain what's really going on with them.

> ***Ephesians 6:12*** – *For we wrestle not against flesh and blood, but against principalities, against powers, against the rulers of the darkness of this world, against spiritual wickedness in high places.*

Although there may be physical evidence of a struggle or challenge, the majority of what we are dealing with stems from the spirit realm. This is difficult to understand at times because something is happening in the spiritual realm that we know nothing about naturally because the unknown can be a downright scary concept, but I am convinced that our spiritual minds know more than we allow ourselves to tap into. I come to find out that most people who are impacted in the spiritual realm in a great way are the ones that have a strong purpose in the earth to fulfill. You better believe that there are all kinds of spiritual forces trying to prevent us from reaching our destiny. We know them as demonic spirits, imps or the devil himself. The Bible gives the devil and his cohorts many names but we must read the Bible if we want to know all their names. Do not despair because God has given us power and He's even giving us angels to fight on our behalf.

> ***Luke 10:19*** - *Behold, I give unto you power to tread on serpents and scorpions, and over all the power of the*

enemy: and nothing shall by any means hurt you.

When my son was growing up, before we would leave our apartment every morning, we would stand by the door and I would hold his hands and pray the following:

Dear Heavenly Father, please watch over my son and myself as we travel to and fro. Thank you for watching over all of our loved ones; LORD please release our angels of protection to fight off any seen or unseen danger. Thank you for keeping us and all of our loved ones safe from any harm and danger. I bind up the enemy on every hand and I come against any retaliation or backlash spirit, we plead the Blood of Jesus over us right now in Jesus Mighty name. Amen.

We believe in our prayers because the Bible tells us to come boldly to His throne of grace and that we can be confident that whatever we ask Him that He is able to perform it. God gives us angels and they work for us. We can ask our angels to protect us and I believe that they will do just that.

> ***Psalm 91:11*** *– For he shall give his angels charge over thee, to keep thee in all thy ways.*

Faith is important to have as the Christian believer. I understand that we are all on different faith levels, as the Bible lets us know that we grow from faith to faith. The more we know about the Lord, this helps us to believe and trust in the Lord. This faith or trust helps us to become strong in our Christian walk with the Lord. Faith also helps us to be strong in many situations.

> ***Ephesians 3:20*** *– Now unto him that is able to do exceeding abundantly above all that we ask or think, according to the power that worketh in us.*

That power that we possess is our faith and our faith grows as we exercise it by believing God's Word, trusting what He says and obeying Him. There are many components to faith. At its most simplistic form, faith is a fruit of the Spirit as well as a gift (Ephesians 6, 1 Corinthians 12). The Bible lets us know that we go from faith to faith, which simply means that our faith grows and advances in stages and levels. God has given all us *the measure of faith* (Romans 12:3). I don't know exactly what a measure of faith is but I do know that every believer has faith because God has given it to us. Just like we turn on the light – it's up to us to turn our faith on to activate it.

If ye have faith as a grain of mustard seed, ye shall say unto this mountain, Remove hence to yonder place; and it shall remove; and nothing shall be impossible unto you (Matthew 17:20). Our faith can help us to be strong and our faith can help us to get through the most challenging parts of this life. There are no shortcuts. Some people learn this earlier in life and some at later stages of their life but no matter where you are, it's never too late to allow your faith to grow.

I remember a song we used to sing when I was little girl. "Lord, don't move this mountain but give me strength to climb." Some mountains (problems, issues, etc.) may not immediately move but you will need God's strength and His ability to make it through. Here's a quote people use often, "I'm coming up the rough side of the mountain." My friend always say that if it was a smooth mountain, you would not have anything to grip or hold on to and it would be impossible to climb. I guess what I'm saying rough mountains are not impossible to climb and rough mountains are good for increasing endurance and strength. Rough mountains help develop our character.

> *Character cannot be developed in ease and quiet. Only through experience of trial and suffering can the soul be strengthened, vision cleared, ambition inspired, and success achieved.*
>
> *– **Helen Keller***

Ephesians 5:26-27 let us know that God is *making us holy by washing us with the Word*. He wants us to be clean, as white as snow, without stain or wrinkle or any other blemish. Suffering develops holiness in unholy people. But getting there is painful while undergoing the cleansing in the Lord's "laundry room." When you use bleach to get rid of stains, it's a harsh process. Getting rid of wrinkles are even more painful: ironing means a combination of heat plus pressure. Ouch! No wonder suffering hurts!

What I love about Ephesians 3:20 is that this scripture points out that *God is able to do exceeding abundantly above all that we ask or think according to the power that is in us.* I know from personal experience that this scripture is true. Nothing or no one can take away the faith that I have in God. I give my Mom a big shout out for teaching us about Jesus as babies. I can remember as early as three years of age knowing who Jesus is. Jesus was part of our family as much as my mother, father, brothers, and sister were part of the family.

My father and mother passed away 11 months apart when I was 18 and 19 years of age. I found that what they instilled in us about faith in God is what carried me through those dark days of coping with their deaths. When my father passed away I was in college, 300 miles from home in a town named Carthage I still had shelter over my head at the dormitory so I didn't have to think about where I was going to live or what I was going to eat, but the pain almost felt unbearable. I could hardly think. Being this young and now without my earthly father, the father that I watched the Cubs with the father that took me to see wrestling, the father that read to me; the burden was too heavy to carry.

I remember the day I got the phone call that my father had made his transition. I was lying in the bed. As a matter of fact, I didn't attend any of my classes that day. I was feeling and acting weird. I wasn't hungry. I had lost my appetite. I laid in the bed all day, unable to sleep, unable to eat. I just had this weird feeling. I can remember one of my classmates coming into my room and asking me what was wrong and if I had notified the school that I wasn't going to attend any of my classes that day. Needless to say, I did not call anybody and I did not plan on calling anyone.

My faithful classmate called in for me, knowing that I had never missed class. I remember her asking me, "Are you sick? What is wrong?" I told her, "No, I'm not sick. I'm not hungry and I do not know what is wrong. All I know is that I want to be left alone." She obliged and left my room in a hurry.

My father was up in age when I was conceived. At the time of my conception, my father was already 55 years of age. When he made his transition, he was 73 years of age.

The image and memory that is very vivid in my mind is of a time when I was about five years of age. I can remember the sun was shining and it was Summer My father and I were walking around the side of the building where we lived. He was holding my hand and I could remember being so happy and realizing that I should cherish that moment. I did cherish that moment that day, and I still cherish that moment today.

I took the train home so that I could attend my father's funeral. I remember sitting in the train station feeling all alone and wanting to die. This was the first time I ever felt like I wanted to die. I wanted to be with my father. I exited the train station and deliberately walked down the block where my boyfriend at that time lived. As I approached my boyfriend's house, there he was standing on the porch. Although we had not spoken yet since my father passed away, he already knew what had happened because at the time my father was making his transition, he had called the house and heard all the commotion over my father. I learned later that he called at the same exact time that my father was making his transition.

My father died and months later I find out that I am pregnant, seven months pregnant to be exact. I am "kind of" living with and visiting with my sister in Lynwood, California. It happens again. I'm lying in the bed all day, unable to sleep, unable to eat, unable to do anything that would take will power and thought.

My sister keeps asking me, "What is wrong?" I tell her I do not know. My sister tries to encourage me to eat for the baby's sake, but I told her I can't. I'm not hungry. For some reason, the phone was disconnected, and there is a knock at the door. At the door, there is a man delivering a telegram. My sister and I open the telegram, which was sent by my sister in Chicago, Illinois. The telegram notifies us that our mother had passed away.

I'm pregnant, unmarried, and broke in California. "I'm not even married or living with my baby daddy". Reality begins to set in.

I head back home to Chicago, Illinois for my mother's funeral. It felt like the bus trip home was the longest bus ride ever. What am I going to do now? Even though my mother was sick and in a convalescent home, she was still my mother. You can go to your mother for any and everything. Now, my mother is, also, gone.

My mother was almost 18 years younger than my father. My mother was only 56 years of age when she passed away. She was not that old. Well, the closer I get to that age, 56 does not seem so old anymore!

While I faced many difficult times after this, God showed up in my life, seemingly just in the nick of time. No matter what I had to endure, I made a choice and decision that I will endure *difficulties as a good soldier* (2 Timothy 2:3-5).

What I found out through life's journey is that soldiers do not throw their weapons down on the battlefield no matter how fierce the battle may become. True soldiers may get wounded in battle, and true soldiers may even die on the battlefield, but a true soldier will never quit. A true soldier is not born with a special gene that automatically makes him a good soldier. It is only through training, discipline, and a sheer will to develop his craft and maximize his skill that he grows to become a truly good soldier.

The school of life reflects this design as well. After making it through the boot camp of life, one becomes a true soldier. I believe that the life lessons we learn are a form of boot camp for Christians. Just as a soldier starts out in boot camp to learn endurance and to build their body and mental strength, the same goes for the Christian. However, our boot camp is life.

For the soldier, boot camp is basic training in the armed forces. Boot camp (basic training) is designed to lay a foundation for discipline and basic combat. Discipline is merely instructions. Basic combat is warfare. Christians must also open their ears, hearts, and souls to discipline and instruction. However, the instructions do not come from a drill sergeant, Christian instructions comes from the Captain of our soul.

Christians have to engage in warfare too. A few scriptures come to mind. The first one is *Psalm 144:1*, where David, a warrior and king, proclaims *Blessed be the Lord my strength which teacheth my hands to war, and my fingers to fight*. Although King David engaged in physical combat, the fight of Christians today isn't against flesh and blood, but against principalities.

> ***Ephesians 6:12*** – *For we wrestle not against flesh and blood, but against principalities, against powers, against the rulers of the darkness of this world, against spiritual wickedness in high places.*

Just as a soldier in boot camp has to exercise to build mental and physical endurance, Christians also will have to build their spirituality by exercising their faith.

When the Apostle Paul was at the end of his ministry, he wrote a letter to encourage Timothy. One thing Paul told Timothy (I imagine Paul with much excitement)*is I have fought a good fight, I have finished my course, I have kept the faith* (2 Timothy 4:7). Yes, Christians have to contend and fight for your faith. This is one of the biggest fights that Christians will have in this life. Fighting for one's faith is not the only fight that Christians will have, but it is one of the biggest fights Christians will have.

Paul continued to encourage Timothy. He later tells Timothy to endure hardness as a good soldier. Paul didn't sugar coat life, ministry, or misery. He tells Timothy to *be steadfast unmovable; always abounding in the work of the Lord for as much as you know your labor is not in vain* (1 Corinthians 15:58).

How wonderful to know that no matter what, we must endure. No matter what life throws at us, no matter what the devil tries to do, our labor is NOT in vain. No matter how many hurts, how many difficult situations, how many setbacks we may experience, our work for the LORD will one day bear fruit, be rewarded, and earn each of us a crown of life. What a Mighty God we serve!

You will know when you have the strength and fortitude to endure the harshness of life and the battles of evil as a good soldier because not only will you no longer have a give-up mentality, you will not quit. Philippians 4:13 will resonate in your soul: *I can do all things through Christ which strengtheneth me.* This simple statement reveals that again, we will not have to go through the hurt, the pain, and any obstacle by ourselves because the Lord will always be with us.

Broken Beyond Belief

When I suffered loss after loss and went through difficult situations, I used to cry a lot. Actually, I was the last born, the baby in the family. I used to get with God and downright throw all kinds of tantrums. And one day, God sent me a vision of a baby dressed in just a diaper and lying on his back on a battlefield. The baby was kicking and screaming profusely. While the baby was lying on his back, kicking, and screaming, bullets were flying around the baby. The Spirit of the Lord spoke quietly to my spirit and said the battlefield is no place for a baby. Right then and there in that moment, I began to grow up. Childish play, thoughts, and actions were over for me.

Life was happening, and it was happening fast. Now, I was getting ready to birth a child into this world. I will never forget my father or mother, but I knew that they were not coming back no matter how many tantrums I threw. The good thing for me is that I always read the Bible even from the time of being a little girl. I know that the Bible is where I get a lot of my strength from - the Word of God.

Remember that our struggle is against spiritual wickedness in high places and as the Apostle Paul states our struggle as humans is to walk in the Spirit.

> ***Galatians 5:16-18*** *– This I say then, Walk in the Spirit, and ye shall not fulfil the lust of the flesh. ¹⁷ For the flesh lusteth against the Spirit, and the Spirit against the flesh: and these are contrary the one to the other: so that ye cannot do the things that ye would. ¹⁸ But if ye be led of the Spirit, ye are not under the law.*

So, how do we walk in the Spirit? Baby allowing the Holy Spirit to produce His fruit in us so that no matter what we face, we will have what we need to be successful on this Christian journey and to have victory after victory.

> ***Galatians 6:22-25*** *– But the fruit of the Spirit is love, joy, peace, longsuffering, gentleness, goodness, faith, ²³ Meekness, temperance: against such there is no law. ²⁴*

And they that are Christ's have crucified the flesh with the affections and lusts. 25 If we live in the Spirit, let us also walk in the Spirit.

We are to live and walk in the Spirit. Walk is a verb. It's an action word. Walking in the Spirit means that if we are living in the Spirit, we should be able to demonstrate some type of maturity in our daily lives. Am I saying that Christians are perfect? No, not at all, but what I am saying is that we should always grow in our faith.

When we first start out on our Christian journey, think of a little baby who must first learn how to crawl before he or she will be able to walk. We may even start out crawling but as we continue to nourish ourselves in the word and love of God by regularly attending church services and faithfully reading the Bible, we will find ourselves growing in the admonition of the Lord.

__I Corinthians 13: 11__ – When I was a child, I spake as a child, I understood as a child, I thought as a child: but when I became a man, I put away childish things.

Just as the Apostle Paul said when he was child, he *spake* as child. There comes a time in every Believer's life when they will begin to grow spiritually. When we feast on the Word of God and His precepts, we can't help but begin to grow and mature. There comes a time in all of us where child's play is over.

> **1 Peter 2:2** – *As newborn babes, desire the sincere milk of the Word, that ye may grow thereby:*

A person does not grow into becoming a Christian. Conversion is an instantaneous miracle. The new birth is a sudden occurrence in the life of a Believer. The moment he or she exercises faith in Christ, he is placed into the body of Christ. It is not a process. It is a spectacular, immediate miracle. There may be a process of exposing someone to the gospel, but the actual point of salvation occurs in a miraculous moment. The believer passes from death into life, "*from the power of darkness...into the kingdom of His Dear Son*" (Colossians 1:13).

Spiritual growth is not a question of our position in Christ because we were placed in Christ the moment we put our faith in Him. Once we verbally confess and believe in our heart that Jesus Christ is Lord, we are converted to a Christian, a Believer and follower of Christ.

Although becoming a Christian is an instantaneous miracle, we still have to grow spiritually. As Paul said, we are to desire sincere milk as a newborn baby; we are not expected to stop in one day our dependence on milk for nourishment and growth. Just as a newborn baby grows, we grow spiritually and begin to digest solid spiritual food.

> **2 Peter 3:18** – *But grow in grace, and in the knowledge of our Lord and Savior, Jesus Christ.*

God has given us assistance by way of the Bible, the Holy Ghost, grace and His mercy. Grace is God's loving kindness that we do not deserve nor can we ever earn, but God gives us His grace to help us on our Christian journey.

God knows that we're imperfect people but we're not to use our imperfections as a crutch (e.g. deliberately not do something or do something wrong and say God knows my heart). Whatever area in our lives that we can improve upon, we need to do so with all discipline and diligence because, truth be told, God knows our hearts and that's why He sent us help through our Lord and Savior Jesus Christ.

God also knows that each day we need to start with a fresh clean slate; therefore, He gives us *brand new mercies every morning* (Lamentations 3:22). I would end my night with a prayer of thanksgiving to the Lord and a prayer of repentance where I may have fallen short or even missed the mark. In the morning, I wake up with prayers of gratitude for watching over me, my love ones, family, friends and often thanks to Him for His brand-new mercies and starting my day by directing my path.

> **Lamentations 3:22-23** – *It is of the Lord's mercies that we are not consumed, because his compassions fail not.* [23] *They are new every morning: great is thy faithfulness.*

There are many people have been saved for a long period of time but have grown very little. Many people have been saved for a brief period of time and have grown a great deal. Certainly, time is a factor in spiritual growth for some. However, the amount of time isn't what is important; it is a commitment to the principles of growth in God that makes the difference. We don't measure spiritual maturity by the calendar.

Some people think that if they have been active in the church for a while, then they have grown spiritually. In other words, if you are busy, you must be spiritual. But the Pharisees were busy in religion, and no one was further from the truth than they were. In Matthew 7:22-23, Jesus said, *"Many will say to Me in that day, Lord, Lord, have we not...done many wonderful works? And then will I profess unto them, I never knew you; depart from me...."* Being busy doesn't even qualify someone for salvation yet alone spiritual growth.

At times, we equate spiritual maturity with what we know, but that is not the key either. Knowledge alone is not enough. Knowledge is only power when we apply it. The Bible says in 1 Corinthians 8:1 ...*Knowledge puffeth up, but charity edifieth.* When a Believer becomes prideful, spiritual growth is immediately retarded. Having knowledge of facts cannot be equated with spiritual maturity. Only when those facts conform us to the image of Christ does our knowledge relate to our growth. Further what offsets or balances out pride is the love that we have for Christ, ourselves and for others; whether they are believers or non-believers, whether they are family members or friends, whether they are enemies for the Bible says we have to love our enemies too.

It's only when our self-image becomes more like Christ, then and only then can we begin to measure our Christian growth and maturity. The more we become like Christ, the more we will see our own errors and faults. Our focus will be on our own spiritual growth. We will still love, pray, and rebuke others, but we will be more concerned about pleasing the Lord and doing things God's way. Slowly, God's desires will become our desires.

Certainly, the things we succumb to last year should not be the same things that we succumb to today. There should be some growth in our daily lives, but do not make the mistake of comparing one's self to any other person as progress is made on one's Christian journey. If there are any comparisons, it should be that of comparing one's self to Christ. One person's struggle may not be another person's struggle; and one person's struggle may not be the struggle of another person because each person is individually and uniquely created by God.

A butterfly did not come here as a butterfly, but it went through several stages of metamorphosis. Just as the butterfly did not begin its life as a beautiful butterfly, a Christian's journey does not begin easy or beautiful. This is why Paul tells us *therefore if any man be in Christ, he is a new creature: old things are passed away; behold, all things are become new (2 Corinthians 5:17)*. God does not want to improve upon us or even make us better; God wants to make us altogether new.

When we become new creatures in Christ, the old way of living, the old way of thinking, and the old way of doing things (i.e. if it's not of God or like Christ) are changed because the Holy Spirit that dwells inside of us is changing us into the person or being who God wants us to be. Transforming not into who we think we should be; not into who our friends, mother, or father say that we should be, but we are changing into who God has created us to be before the foundation of this world. The LORD let Jeremiah know that He had anointed him before the foundation of the earth (Jeremiah 1:11). Before the blueprint of earth was in Heaven, God knew us. God created us for such a time as this. God has a purpose on this earth for each living soul, whether we fulfill our God given purpose or not.

> ***Ephesians 1:4*** – *According as He hath chosen us in him before the foundation of the world, that we should be holy and without blame before him in love...*

Before the world was made, God had already chosen us to be His and chosen us to be holy and without fault before Him. When I hear the word "chosen" and that God chose me, this makes me feel pretty special.

I remember the first time I heard that I was chosen by God. My pastor told me this many years ago. I felt pretty special then. I still feel special because I know beyond a shadow of doubt that I am truly chosen by God, and that's the same assurance that God wants each person to have. Being chosen by God does not make us perfect, but we are growing in His grace. Ephesians 1:4 let us know that we are to be without blame. This does not mean we are perfect, but we should strive for perfection.

God knows that we were born in sin and shaped in iniquity. God also knew that we needed a Savior, which God sent His only begotten Son. God also knows that we are not perfect people. However, God has given us everything that we need to become successful Christians. God has helped us by giving us the Holy Ghost to comfort, strengthen, and to teach us. God has also given His mercy and His grace to assist us. This is God's unmerited love and undeserved favor.

Even when we miss the mark, fall short, and sin, God has given us an opportunity to repent. There's a word for you: repent. Repent means to regret the wrong thing that you've done **AND** to turn away from any sin that may be present in your life and then cry out to the Lord. Let God know your regrets and ask for forgiveness. Repenting should not be a once in a lifetime occurrence, but it should be an immediate response each time we miss the mark. When we miss the mark, we should ask the Lord to provide us with the strength to live a righteous life. He will do just that.

I hear some people saying, "Once saved, always saved." I don't really believe this. Those who believe this generally do not repent when they sin. They feel like everything is covered under the Blood of Jesus. We must understand that sin leads us away from the Lord, and sin undealt with leads us even further away from the Lord.

> **Hebrews 10:29** *(MSG) –   If we give up and turn our backs on all we've learned, all we've been given, all the truth we now know, we repudiate Christ's sacrifice and are left on our own to face the Judgment—and a mighty fierce judgment it will be! If the penalty for breaking the Law of Moses is physical death, what do you think will happen if you turn on God's Son, spit on the sacrifice that made you whole, and insult this most gracious Spirit? This is no light matter. God has warned us that he'll hold us to account and make us pay. He was quite explicit: "Vengeance is mine, and I won't*

overlook a thing" and "God will judge his people." Nobody's getting by with anything, believe me.

Jeremiah 3:14 *– Turn, O backsliding children, saith the Lord; for I am married unto you...*

I know that many quote the scripture that the Lord is married to the backslider. These persons feel like the Lord will never leave or divorce you. This may be true. The Lord may never divorce you, but that doesn't mean that you won't leave or divorce the Lord. God already let us know in His Word, how can two walk together unless they agree? You cannot agree with God and the world at the same time. The world represents sin. Jesus informed us that *no man can serve two masters because you will love one and hate the other* (Matthew 6:24).

It's just impossible to love the Lord and love the world too. There's no way you will know the Lord as your personal Lord and Savior and not give up or want to give up your worldly desires. Worldly desires are indicative of sin too. That's why Jesus told us to come out from amongst them.

Are Christians better than the people in the world? No, of course not! A Christian is a repentant sinner. The difference is one repented and the other one did not. The Christian is in good standing with the Lord and the other one is not in good standing with the Lord. The Christian is Heaven bound and the unrepentant sinner is hell bound. Excuse my directness, but the truth will set you free. Agree?

The flip side to being repentant is that some people think that they can sin effortlessly and repent without ever growing in the grace of the Lord. This is not true.

> ***Galatians 5:22-23*** *– But the fruit of the Spirit is love, joy, peace, longsuffering, gentleness, goodness, faith,* [23] *Meekness, temperance: against such there is no law.*

As previously mentioned, to live a life of righteousness and holiness, we must walk in the Spirit and to help us do that, God has given us *the fruit of the Spirit* Two important factors to remember are:

1) That these are ONLY some of the fruit of the Spirit that are listed here, there are other fruit of the Spirit listed in the Bible;

2) The fruit of the Spirit has to be cultivated in our lives in order to see a real manifestation in our lives.

For example, if we need to grow in love we will find ourselves around hard or difficult to love people. If we need more joy in our lives, we may find ourselves having to deal with sorrowful situations. Suffering can help us to produce patience in our lives. Suffering also can help us to endure hardships that may arise in our lives; to mature in the things of God; and to develop a closeness to the Lord to trust God.

Patience (longsuffering) helps us to endure through the storms of life (tests, trials and temptations) long enough to trust God. Suffering can show up when a boss is treating you unfairly, a spouse has a short fuse, a parent or a child may be at odds with each other. Unless we cultivate opportunities to put into practice this kind of patience, we will not be able to allow suffering or patience to do the work in us that needs to be done.

Let suffering have her perfect work in you. Suffering brings about patience, and this patience also brings about endurance. Remember, we just talked about being able to endure hardness as a good soldier. Endurance helps us to trust in God while we wait on Him to answer our prayers. We develop a closeness to God in and during our suffering when we trust God for the outcome. Whether the outcome is favorable or unfavorable, our trust is in God and God alone. Have faith like the Hebrew boys who were threatened to be thrown into a fiery furnace if they did not fall down and worship the golden calf. All three Hebrew boys answered the king with the same confidence. They told the king that "our God will deliver us and if He doesn't deliver - God is still God" (Daniel 3).

The outcome of our situations or stories does not change who God is. God will forever sit on the throne. Hardships can show up in our home, on our jobs, in our community, and sometimes even in the church.

Matthew 26:41 – *Watch and pray, that ye enter not into temptation: the spirit indeed is willing, but the flesh is weak.*

Why is the flesh so weak? David tells us in Psalm 51:5 that we were *shapen in iniquity and born into sin.* The Apostle Paul also stated that when he would do good that the very presence of evil was there. This evil did not show up from other people or an outside force. Paul was talking about the sin that was already inside of himself.

> **Romans 7:18-20** – *For I know that in me (that is, in my flesh,) dwelleth no good thing: for to will is present with me; but how to perform that which is good I find not. 19 For the good that I would I do not: but the evil which I would not, that I do. 20 Now if I do that I would not, it is no more I that do it, but sin that dwelleth in me.*

The minute we were born, our flesh knew sin. Why? In the Garden of Eden where Adam and Eve resided, they knew no sin until they ate the forbidden fruit off the tree of Knowledge of good and evil. From the beginning of time, God never intended for man to die; however, God has made an escape path for His people.

Adam and Eve were spiritual beings (which is comprised of our mind, will and emotions), who were created to never experience death. As result of sin, God put flesh on their spiritual bodies, and that's why flesh has to go through the transitioning of death. *The wages of sin is death but the gift of God is eternal life* (Romans 6:23). God's gift to the human race is His Son, Jesus Christ, who came to redeem us from death.

> ***Ephesians 2:8*** *– For by grace are ye saved through faith; and that not of yourselves: it is the gift of God:*

As we can see, another one of our biggest fights is not with other people but it's within ourselves. The fight we have is with sin. We struggle with many things…on our jobs, in our home, and even in the church. Sometimes you can find it difficult to be nice to a certain person or people in general, but you know it's the right thing to do. Some people call it biting the bullet or taking the high road, but it's simply being humble. If I said every thought that came to mind, I probably wouldn't have many friends or more importantly. I would be in big trouble with God OFTEN!

> ***Hebrews 12:1 -2*** *— Wherefore seeing we also are compassed about with so great a cloud of witnesses, let us lay aside every weight, and the sin which doth so easily beset us, and let us run with patience the race that is set before us, 2 Looking unto Jesus the author and finisher of our faith; who for the joy that was set before him endured the cross, despising the shame, and is set down at the right hand of the throne of God.*

Sin can trip us up and get us off track. The Bible tells us that *sin has its pleasures for a season* (Hebrews 11:25). How many know that seasons change? Just as the seasons change here on Earth, when it is time for change in our lives, we too need to make the necessary changes and/or corrections in our lives.

> ***Matthew 16:25-27*** *— For whosoever will save his life shall lose it: and whosoever will lose his life for my sake shall find it. 26 For what is a man profited, if he shall gain*

the whole world, and lose his own soul? or what shall a man give in exchange for his soul? 27 For the Son of man shall come in the glory of his Father with his angels; and then he shall reward every man according to his works.

If we care more about obtaining things in this life than allowing God to be first in our lives, then the very thing that we adore is the very thing that we will lose and vice-versa. When we are more concerned about pleasing God than pleasing our flesh, we gain rewards in Heaven because where your heart is, that is where your treasure will be.

I am sure I am not alone when I say the biggest enemy within me is my thoughts.

Romans 3:23-24 – *For all have sinned, and come short of the glory of God; 24 Being justified freely by his grace through the redemption that is in Christ Jesus.*

God is just. God is a fair and loving God. Just as we all have sinned and fallen short of God's glory, we are saved by God's grace through what we believe (faith) about God's grace. God provided us a way of escape, but an escape from what? From sin, from an eternal death and from a place called hell, a place of eternal suffering and damnation. *For the wages of sin is death* (Romans 6:23). This is not only a physical death, but also an eternal death, a spiritual death, a death that lasts forever and ever and living separated from God. I cannot imagine living out all of eternity separated from my Father in Heaven. Sin separates us from the Father. That is why Jesus (while hanging on the cross) cried out in a loud voice, *"MY GOD, MY GOD, WHY HAS THY FORSAKEN FOR ME?"*

> ***Mark 15:34*** – *Jesus cried with a loud voice, saying,* ***Eloi, Eloi, lama sabachthani?*** *which is, being interpreted, My God, my God, why hast thou forsaken me?*

Jesus took on your sin, my sin, the sins of the world. He died a horrible death. Jesus was tortured. He was spat upon. He was mocked. He was executed. He died for us while we were sinners. Although, Jesus died for us while we were sinners, Jesus did not mean for us to continue to sin. God forbid it. He did it to save us from eternal destruction so that we will not have to experience everlasting life without our Father in Heaven.

I told you about the penalty we must pay for sin and an everlasting spiritual death. There are no second chances. There are no do overs, but there is the gift of God.

Romans 6:23 – *For the wages of sin is death; but the gift of God is eternal life through Jesus Christ our Lord.*

When someone offers you a gift, you have to accept the gift for there to be value. The gift that God offers to the entire world is Salvation through Jesus. For this gift to work in our lives, we must accept this gift of life.

Accepting Jesus as our Personal Lord and Savior simply means that we believe that Jesus died for our sins. We believe that the Word of God is from God and that God's Word is true and endures forever. When we, as

Christians, make the transition from this life on Earth, we go to our Father in Heaven.

Knowing this has helped me to cope with death a little bit better knowing that *to be absent from the body is to be present with the LORD* (2 Corinthians 5:6). For my love ones that have accepted Jesus as their Personal Lord and Savior, they have already made their transition. I know that I will see them again and that brings me great joy and peace.

> ***1 Corinthians 15:55*** – *O death, where is thy sting? O grave, where is thy victory?*

As I mentioned above, I do not believe that our souls ever die. I believe this because of a near death experience that I had when I was about nine years of age. My sister and I were at a day camp facility. I thought that I knew how to swim, but quickly learned otherwise. After the third unsuccessful attempt of trying to grab hold to my sister's hand, I began to sink down to the bottom of the pool. I drowned. I saw what I thought was a vision of my funeral; however, it was not my funeral. It was the funeral of my cousin, who was murdered outside of his house on the same day of my drowning.

I remembered my life flashing before my eyes. I got a glimpse of everything that I had done in my life. Since I was only nine years old, everything went by super-fast. Somewhere during this life-flashing experience, I could no longer hear any sounds back here on Earth; such as the water, and children laughing. I heard NOTHING. There was absolute silence, but I remember hearing a voice saying, "I am dead. I am really dead. I also thought that I should be afraid, but I was not afraid. Now, I know that the mind and soul are one and the same, and the soul never dies.

Bible Dictionary: Definition of Soul. The soul is the part of the makeup of every person that is alternately known as the **mind, heart, life,** self, person, or inner being. These are all synonyms for this part of our being. God created us as three-part beings: spirit, soul/mind, and body. www.seekfind.net/Soul.html

There was a real sense of peace. There was so much peace in fact, it kept the fear out. Then, I could feel my spirit moving like it was swimming and traveling somewhere, but I didn't know where. I began to move through this darkness (what felt like a tunnel). Finally, I returned to Earth. A man in the swimming pool helped bring me back to Earth by giving me mouth-to-mouth resuscitation. I thank God for allowing that nice man to resuscitate me; bringing me back to life. I know it was God who allowed that drowning to take place and orchestrated my rescue. So, I must give God honor because without God there would be no life.

I believe the Lord allowed that near-death experience because I used to be so afraid of dying. I was downright terrified of dying. I accidently saw an older lady making her transition when I was a child about five years of age. I will never forget the experience. I was with my sister-in-law, and the woman was someone who my sister-in-law was acquainted with. However, I did not know this lady. She was not a known family member of mine either. I vividly remember that the woman's transition was not silent. It was not pretty. As matter of fact, it was pointblank scary. I will never forget the memory. She was an older lady and very skinny. She probably was not as tall as she appeared to be at the time, but because I was so young she seemed very tall.

I remember standing in a doorway with many other people. I could barely see what was going on because of the crowd of people, but I was finally able to find a spot where I could peek through the crowd and see the lady laying down, as if she were asleep. but All of sudden, thing began to happen. The woman jumped up, grabbed a hammer, and started swinging. Yes, she did. I heard someone ask "what is she doing?" Someone replied that "she was fighting death." That was all I needed to see and hear. Then, someone else shouted get these kids out of here. The kids, including me, were rushed to the porch outside of the house. I still remember it was hot and turning dark out so it must have been in the summer time.

Fighting death was a horrible sight. I didn't really know what was going on then, but now I clearly understand the fight she was in and, unfortunately, it appears that she lost. She lost not because she died. Hebrews 9:27 lets us know that *it is appointed unto men once to die, but after this the judgment*; she lost because her soul was lost. *3*

John 1:2 Beloved, I wish above all things that thou mayest prosper and be in health, even as thy soul prospereth.

Why do our souls need to prosper? Souls never die, and our souls need to be saved. The reason why souls can never die is God breathed a part of Himself into man. Man became a LIVING SOUL. Therefore, if God can never die, neither can we. We can only make a choice of where we would like to spend eternity.

***Genesis 2:7** – And the Lord God formed man of the dust of the ground, and breathed into his nostrils the breath of life; and man became a living soul.*

***James 1:21** (AMP) – So get rid of all uncleanness and all that remains of wickedness, and with a humble spirit receive the word [of God] which is implanted [actually rooted in your heart], which is able to save your souls.*

> **1 Corinthians 15:45** *(AMP) – So it is written [in Scripture], "The first man, Adam, became a living soul (an individual);" the last Adam (Christ) became a life-giving spirit [restoring the dead to life].*

Remember, we wrestle not against flesh and blood but against principalities, spiritual wickedness, and more. God can only help us if we allow Him to help us. No one can come to the Father but by His Son Jesus.

I hear people saying that there are many paths to God. I am not afraid to admit that I do not understand this statement because the Bible clearly lets us know that Jesus is that door and rightfully so. In *John 14:6 Jesus saith unto him, I am the way, the truth, and the life: no man cometh unto the Father, but by Me.*

Many paths? There is only one door and that door is Jesus. Maybe, they're saying many paths lead to Jesus. I can see that. We all come from different walks of life. Hopefully the boy, girl, woman, or man that does not know

Jesus pardons their sins is on the right path to meet up with Jesus. Amen.

> ***2 Corinthians 5:7-8*** *– (For we walk by faith, not by sight); 8 We are confident, I say, and willing rather to be absent from the body, and to be present with the Lord.*

When Christians leave this planet, they return to our Heavenly home, to our Father God. I really never understood *Psalm 116: 15 Precious in the sight of the Lord is the death of his saints*. However, when we make that final transition from Earth to Heaven, it is like a child that was on a long trip away from home, returning home to their parents. Wow! God is so gracious to allow us this time and separation away from Him. There are scriptures that say we have fallen asleep in Christ. For clarity purposes, *1 Corinthians 15:18 "...who have fallen asleep in Christ."* Sleep is a temporary state. The Christian spirit never dies and I believe that is why the word sleep is used instead of saying the Christian died. Flesh dies, but the spirit lives forever.

NOW AND LATER

Seasons change and you have to know that some things are for now and some things are for later. I remember when I was a small child; my friend and I would go to the store and buy candy named 'Now & Laters'. The 'Now & Laters' came in many flavors and colors such as lemon (yellow), grape (purple) cherry, strawberry, watermelon (red), apple (green) . There were other colors and flavors too. The meaning behind the Now & Laters was that you eat some now and saved some for later. That candy tasted so good to me. I always had a difficult time trying to save some for later.

My challenge was not only with the candy, but also with life in general. We spend a lot of our lives waiting on things. We wait to go to school. We go to school, and then we wait to graduate. Some of us cannot wait to be married, a millionaire, or work in a particular field. We spend a lot of time waiting on getting to the next level instead of enjoying the moment and the process of obtaining that next goal. We must learn how to live in the moment and enjoy that too.

The Apostle Paul put it best when he said in Philippians 4:12 *I know both how to be abased, and I know how to abound: everywhere and in all things I am instructed both to be full and to be hungry, both to abound and to suffer need*. All Paul was saying is that he had experienced having plenty and times when he did not have enough, but Paul said whatever state he was in, he learned how to be content. We learn from Paul that having more than enough at times and experiencing lack, or whatever the situation may be, God was with him and sustained him. That is where Paul's contentment came from. Through the tough times and the good times, Paul's faith coupled with God's faithfulness allowed Paul to have the confident assurance that no matter what may come his way, God was with him and would provide for him. Paul's satisfaction and contentment was learned through various trials and tribulations.

Nevertheless, I have learned that if we do not have discipline in our lives, we will want all of the good things that life has to offer right now. Waiting is not easy, especially living in today's microwave society where everything happens faster than the speed of light. When you find yourself in the waiting mode, it can become very frustrating. I cannot promise you through the wait that you will not cry or become frustrated or even become discouraged. I know that at times it's not easy to wait on things to happen when you need them to happen immediately or when you want them to happen immediately. God knows that it is not easy to wait and that is why He has left us many amazing scriptures on how to wait and even what type of attitude we should possess while we wait for that special thing to manifest in our lives.

> ***Psalm 27:14*** – *Wait on the LORD: be of good courage, and he shall strengthen thine heart: wait, I say, on the LORD.*

Wait can be the cousin to suffering because both deal with patience. Suffering teaches us to have endurance and endurance teaches us to have patience. We need patience so that we can have the proper attitude while waiting on the Lord to either do something for us, or our loved ones, or to show up in a particular situation that we previously prayed about. Maybe a loved one is battling a chronic illness and needs healing. We pray in faith. We believe God with all of our heart. We know that we trust Him too, but sometimes nothing has happened. There is no miracle. There is no deliverance. In fact, the situation may have worsened. What do you do?

A famous gospel singer said that we should continue to stand. Stand on what? Stand on what we believe. Stand trusting God. Stand knowing that if God did not show up in our situation, that God is still God. God does all things well. When we say that we have faith and believe God to do something for us, we have to believe God enough to release that which we hold dearest in our heart. That means if a love one has to go home to be with the Lord under some unforeseen circumstances, you must trust God that He does all things well. Faith is not about receiving something from God, but faith is being able to release that which we love the most to God.

>*Psalm 37:7* – *Rest in the LORD, and wait patiently for him: fret not thyself because of him who prospereth in his way, because of the man who bringeth wicked devices to pass.*

Sometimes we find ourselves desiring certain things in life, and they seem so farfetched or out of reach, but I believe that longing was placed in our hearts to teach us discipline through delayed gratification. Just because we have not obtained that thing that we hold dearest in our hearts today does not mean we will never achieve or get it. There is an appointed time for all things. We must realize too that whatever that "thing" that we desire in our heart is must be in accordance with the Word of God, which is the will of God.

> **1 John 5:14-15** – *And this is the confidence that we have in him, that, if we ask any thing according to his will, he heareth us:* ¹⁵ *And if we know that he hear us, whatsoever we ask, we know that we have the petitions that we desired of him.*

How do we obtain those desires in our hearts? Simply trusting God enough to believe that He cares enough about us. Expectation. We must not be afraid to expect God to show up when we need Him the most; even if He does not show up with what we think we need the most. Know that God can show up with peace when there is no peace. He can show up with joy when there is no joy. Rest assured, He will show up.

Generally, He shows up through other people. God can move upon a person's heart to help us in many ways not imagined. That is why we have to cross over into the land of expectation.

Matthew 6:33 – But seek ye first the kingdom of God and His righteousness; and all these things shall be added unto you.

Just because we are Christians doesn't mean that we do not have desires in our hearts. Some of the desires that we have in our hearts come from God Himself. We just need to stop, pray, and ask God to direct our path. Ask Him what should be our next step. God already knows what our desires. Remember we are in a relationship with Him, and He wants to hear from us. He wants us to commune (talk) with Him. We may have desires that God placed in our hearts, but that does not mean the road is going to be smooth. There may be bumps in the road and some obstacles. I love to hear a well-known radio personality say, *"the road to success is always under construction."* There are going to be some obstacles, but that doesn't mean we stop building. We must continue to build and watch God honor and reward our faithfulness and diligence. Never allow obstacles, situations, and/or people to discourage us to the point of giving up or quitting. It is a trick from the devil.

> ***Psalm 37:4*** *– Delight thyself also in the LORD: and he shall give thee the desires of thine heart.*

It is time to get happy in the LORD! That is really for the end of this book, but I couldn't help myself! When things do not go our way, we trust that God is still God. After faith and trust, we must be obedient to His will. That does not mean that we are going to become perfect individuals, but God does expect us to mature or grow daily in God.

Again, we do this by forming or developing a relationship with God, spending time in prayer, and reading His Word. If God gives us brand new mercies every morning (Lamentations 3:22-23), it is because He knew that we were going to need them. God loves us enough to send His Son, but He didn't stop there. He continues to supply us with His loving kindness. Do not be confused or misunderstand that we have a license to sin because **we do not**.

We must remember that when we sin, we insult the Spirit of Grace. We do not want to knowingly or unknowingly offend the Spirit of Grace. When we offend the Spirit of Grace, we are rejecting God's help, God's love, and everything that He put in place for us to be successful on this Christian journey.

> ***Hebrews 10: 26-39*** *(VOICE) – Now if we willfully persist in sin after receiving such knowledge of the truth, then there is no sacrifice left for those sins— 27 only the fearful prospect of judgment and a fierce fire that will consume God's adversaries. 28 Remember that those who depart from the Law of Moses are put to death without mercy based on the testimony of two or three witnesses. 29 Just think how much more severe the punishment will be for those who have turned their backs on the Son of God, trampled on the blood of the covenant by which He made them holy, and outraged the Spirit of grace with their*

contempt. ³⁰ For we know the God who said, "Vengeance belongs to Me—I will repay," also said, "The Eternal One will judge His people." ³¹ It is truly a frightening thing to be on the wrong side of the living God. ³² Instead, think back to the days after you were first enlightened and understood who Jesus was: when you endured all sorts of suffering in the name of the Lord, ³³ when people held you up for public scorn and ridicule, or when they abused your partners and companions in the faith. ³⁴ Remember how you had compassion for those in prison and how you cheerfully accepted the seizure of your possessions, knowing that you have a far greater and more enduring possession. ³⁵ Remember this, and do not abandon your confidence, which will lead to rich rewards. ³⁶ Simply endure, for when you have done as God requires of you, you will receive the promise. ³⁷ As the prophet Habakkuk said, In a little while, only a little longer, the One who is coming will come without delay. 38 But My righteous one must live by faith, for if he gives up his commitment, My soul will have no pleasure in him. 39 My friends, we are not those who give up hope and so are lost; but we are of the company who live by faith and so are saved.

Sinning willingly is different from struggling with sin. Let me explain. When I choose to sin because I like what I am doing and I do not want to stop sinning, I do not want to change and I do not want to stop sinning. We have no more Blood Sacrifice for our sins. We do not have a license to sin. Not ONLY do we not have any more of Jesus' Blood, we have insulted the Spirit of Grace. Yes, we talk about God's grace, and we love God's grace, but I think what we forget is that God is the Spirit of Grace. When we choose to do the opposite of what God has laid out for us to do, we are telling the Lord I don't love You. We are telling the Lord that we do not believe and really do not care. When we insult someone, we are treating them with disrespect. When we willingly sin against God, we are willingly disrespecting God (the Spirit of Grace).

> ***Psalm 51:4*** *– Against thee, thee only, have I sinned, and done this evil in thy sight: that thou mightest be justified when thou speakest, and be clear when thou judgest.*

Remember David, the king of Judah, in the royal lineage of our Lord and Savior Jesus Christ, the one after God's own heart. David praised God so much that he danced right out of his outer clothes! Yes, that David, who committed adultery with Uriah's wife Bathsheba and orchestrated a murder on Uriah to cover up the affair that he had with Uriah's wife. What I love about David is that after the LORD revealed the extent of his sin, David did not try to make any excuses. He did not lie and try to cover up or hide what he did. In Psalm 51, David is pleading his case with the LORD. David was guilty as he had committed not one, but two awful sins. God told David that if he would have asked for Bathsheba, God would have giving her to him. Wow! That's food for thought.

If we ask God for something and God does not give it to us, and God says "no," God knows that it is something that we do not need. David pleads with the LORD to create in him a clean heart and renew the right spirit within him. Although David committed adultery and murder, he said, "God, against you and against you alone have I sinned." I believe that when we sin, we think that we are not hurting anyone, but this is the furthest thing from the truth. Get that thing (sin), whatever it is, right with the Lord.

Psalm 51:9 – *Hide thy face from my sins, and blot out all mine iniquities.10 Create in me a clean heart, O God; and renew a right spirit within me.11 Cast me not away from thy presence; and take not thy holy spirit from me.*

No matter what struggle we may experience in our lives, we have to know and believe that God is working it out for our good. No matter how bad it may look, no matter how bad it may feel, we have to know and trust that God is working it out for us. Think about certain situations that you have been through. Maybe you lost a loved one near and dear to your heart, and somebody else was in that same situation, but they did not come out like you did. They may have lost their mind, or they may have lost their very own life. It could have happened to you, but for some reason the Lord did not allow it to happen to you. I don't know what your 'it' is, but do know everybody has an 'it' in their life.

While we are waiting, know that God is also helping us to develop patience. I found that I developed the most endurance from the various trials that I had to go through in my life. I personally do not believe that God causes bad things to happen to people, but I do believe that the Lord allows us to grow through various difficult situations to help us to mature and to become stronger, wiser, and purer.

When God is dealing with us (working), separation brings sanctification. It is a process. There are those times that God does things that we know nothing about. This is the very reason why we cannot lean on our own understanding. We cannot depend on our own thoughts or opinions.

Isaiah 55:8-9 *– For my thoughts are not your thoughts, neither are your ways my ways, saith the Lord. 9 For as the Heavens are higher than the earth,* *so are my ways higher than your ways, and my thoughts than your thoughts.*

As previously mentioned, one of the fruit of the Spirit is suffering. This does not mean to suffer long, that is not God's intention for this fruit, but God does want His people to learn how to be tolerant of certain things and how to endure some of the harshness of this life because God knows that the trials we go through in life not only make us stronger but also help us to become more patient and better people in the midst of adversity. The Bible tells us to *endure hardness as a good soldier* (2 Timothy 2:3). The Bible also tells us to let patience have her perfect work in us.

There is a work that suffering and patience wants to do in us. Suffering wants to establish us in the truth and the light of His word so that we may be able to stand in the midst of any trial and situation.

> ***James 1:1-5** – James, a servant of God and of the Lord Jesus Christ, to the twelve tribes which are scattered abroad, greeting. 2 My brethren, count it all joy when ye fall into divers temptations; 3 Knowing this, that the trying of*

your faith worketh patience. James: 4 But let patience have her perfect work, that ye may be perfect and entire, wanting nothing.

We are not on trial, but our faith is. We do not have to have ever done anything wrong, but our faith must be tested and approved by God. This is why it is necessary to possess the fruit of suffering. Suffering brings patience. Patience brings endurance. Endurance enables us to go through overwhelming situations without crumbling.

God wants us to become mature people. He wants us to grow up and not walk around feeling helpless and hopeless. We see through all of the hard trials that we have had to endure that it was not just by the luck of the draw or by happenstance that some of the bad things and some of the most difficult things happened to us. It was these difficult and uncomfortable things that happened in our lives that really helped us and allowed us to help someone else.

Have you ever been in a situation where you had gone through a terrible ordeal and it might have made you angry at the time, but nevertheless, you made it out of that situation to find yourself in a better place? Ordinarily, you would not have taken that route, but that thing that angered you or that thing that frustrated you is the very thing that God turned around in your favor.

We often hear people say, "Favor ain't fair", but favor is necessary. Ask Joseph about the favor of God (Genesis 39). Joseph was despised by his brothers. Joseph was young. He was a braggadocios teenager. However, Joseph's brothers plotted to murder him, but his older brother, Reuben, talked them into not murdering Joseph. Instead they sold Joseph into slavery.

Joseph is now residing in a strange land with strange people. If that was not bad enough, while working in Potiphar's house, Potiphar's wife decides to lie on Joseph and say that Joseph tried to rape her. Joseph serves a prison sentence of about two years as a result of Potiphar's lie.

No matter where Joseph went, the favor of God went with Joseph. God's Spirit was upon his life. In prison, he was a leader and had privileges. When Joseph came out of prison, he was the second in command to the king as the governor of Egypt. The people could not do anything unless they went through Joseph. Not only was Joseph able to show the king how to be wise and live and prosper while they were experiencing a famine in the land, Joseph was able to help preserve himself and his own family.

What if Joseph had decided, with all of the bad things that happened in his life and all the things that had gone wrong, to just end it all? There were many opportunities for Joseph to give up. I am sure that Joseph went through many lonely nights. I do not even deny the fact that Joseph probably was at times afraid, hurt, and depressed, but he did not let any of those emotions overtake him. Read more about Joseph in Genesis 45.

As we wait on some things to happen in our lives, whether it be for an answer or for some things to change, we must first have confidence that God is working things out on our behalf. As we wait, we know that we should remain faithful to God and trust that God not only hears us, but He will answer our prayer request(s). We just read in one of the scriptures that we are to be of "good courage," which means that we should be brave no matter what we are facing or how difficult or painful the circumstances might be.

I will never forget the words of my pastor when I was in my 20's. I would testify in church, but I would not have much of a testimony. My pastor would always tell me to be encouraged and be of good cheer. I never really understood this until I became older. In spite of the disappointments and the trials in this life, always look to God and trust Him. Even on the cloudiest of days, I now always see the silver lining and the sunshine.

David said in Psalm 40:1 *I waited patiently for the LORD; and he inclined unto me, and heard my cry.* It is obvious that God heard David because whatever David was dealing with he said, "the LORD heard my cry." This statement reveals that the Lord allowed something to manifest in a positive way on David's behalf. When we cry out to the Lord, I believe He will always come to our rescue.

> **Psalm 34:18** – *The LORD is near to those who have a broken heart, And saves such as have a contrite spirit.*

God cannot ignore His people who are broken. Webster's New Collegiate Dictionary defines "broken" in many ways, including, but not limited to: *1. Forcibly fractured or damaged and no longer in one piece or in working order. 2. (of a person) having given up all hope; despairing. Shattered, breached, incomplete, crushed, exhausted, and weakened.*

Generally, when things become broken (forcibly fractured, damaged, no longer in one piece, shattered, breached, incomplete, crushed, exhausted and weakened and/or without hope and in despair) instead of trying to save or repair them, sometimes we tend to throw out the damaged goods. This is also true with people. When things do not work properly or the way that we think that they should, we tend to reject the person. This is true in marriage as well. When the person is damaged, generally they become rejected. When you are rejected, you are no longer needed or of any value to the other person.

If you really think about it, God is the ONLY one that can heal a broken heart. There is no medicine for a broken heart. The doctor cannot write you a prescription for a broken heart. God is the only one who knows how to take the broken pieces and put them back together again, not just healing us, but also making us whole. Although God sits high in the Heavens, the Bible says that He is close to those who are lowly in spirit. As high as God sits, He comes to see about those (His children) who are broken. Whether we accept, know or welcome Jesus as our Personal Lord and Savior, the Bible says that God will not despise a broken spirit and contrite heart. God is Father to ALL creation because He created all of us. God desires to heal every one of their broken hearts.

Anything broken takes time to heal. Just as a broken bone in your body needs time to mend in order to properly heal a broken heart or spirit needs time to heal. I have never had any broken bones, but I have had a torn knee ligament, as I mentioned earlier. However, I know any kind of brokenness inside or outside deals with being damaged, hurt or injured badly. I may have never dealt with any broken bones, but I have dealt with a broken heart.

When we deal with brokenness of our heart, it affects our entire being. Why? Remember Proverbs 23:7 says *for as he thinketh in his heart, so is he: Eat and drink, saith he to thee; but his heart is not with thee.* If a person's mind is not for you, neither will their heart be for you. Whatever is on our mind, good or bad, is going to be in our heart.

When a relationship ends and you know that there is no hope in you getting back together, the best thing to do is to move on. Give yourself time away with the Lord to heal properly. If broken bones or torn ligaments need time to heal, don't you need time to heal? Doesn't your heart need time to heal as well? I believe if you want your heart to heal properly, you need that alone time with the Lord. That doesn't mean that you can never be around other people. This just means that you need to spend more quality time with the Lord so that He can heal you properly. Don't be afraid to spend that alone time with the One who created you, and who knows all about you. God loves you so much that He even knows how many hairs are on your head. Go to Him. (Matthew 10:30). Go to God and make it personal. Go to our Father in Heaven because He is waiting.

We generally come to a crossroads in our lives when we go so long on our own fuel (doing things our own way) and do not ever seek the Lord for His help or even giving the Lord the opportunity to heal or to help us. We look to other people to become what God wants to become in our lives and as we continue to seek out other relationships, other friendships, moving from church to church, jobs, family members, etc., we only find that we keep getting back into the same predicament. We will find that we may keep attracting the same type of people and this isn't happening because everyone is bad or that we are bad judges of character. Sometimes God may be trying to tell us something. And, maybe there are times when God is trying to do something in our lives.

If you find yourself alone, angry, and without hope, God wants to fill those cracks with His love, joy, and peace. As my friend Sherwin always say, "We all have cracks in our clay, but I'm so glad that God is the Potter and we are the clay. The Potter wants to put you back together again." Let God aggrandize those cracks by filling those cracks with His precious love. Let God build you in the power that you need to live this life, the power to be healed, the power to be made whole, the power to not give up, and the power to move forward.

God draws us in. He calls us. He longs for us to come to Him so He can heal us. Can you imagine a parent that knows their child is struggling and in trouble and wants to help, but cannot help because the child will not allow the parent to help them? Often, we are unable to hear God's call because we are so busy with other things – our lives, our families, our work, our own problems and unhappiness. Sometimes we must be broken before we realize our need and God's need. Our deepest need is to be reconciled to God. Only then can we be made whole (Matthew 5:5).

The solution can never come from our own efforts. Similar to the broken bone that grows a callous around it to help it mend, we too can grow a callous around our heart if we do not allow the Lord to heal us properly. Remember, we are to *guard our hearts because out of it flows the issues of life*. Those issues that we have not dealt with can flow out of our heart, and we then find ourselves swimming in anger and drowning in hurt. This is why it is necessary to allow God to heal us properly.

Only when we recognize our need for God are we able to take our eyes off ourselves and focus them on God and Jesus Christ. When we stop thinking about ourselves and start thinking about what Jesus did for us, we begin to heal. When we admit our needs and invite God into our lives, God will begin to make us whole. When we confess that we are broken, God will make us into what He wants us to be. Once we let go of self and place God at the center of our lives, everything else falls into place (Matthew 6:33).

Think about it. Jesus became broken on the cross so that He could heal us in every broken area of our lives.

Salvation was the main part of Jesus being crucified on the cross, but Jesus' work did not stop on Calvary's cross. Why would you choose to stay broken, helpless, hurt and/or injured when you could be made whole?

JESUS came to heal the broken hearted and to preach deliverance. He came to restore sight to the blind. I was once blind "spiritually", but now I can see things in God's light, the way God sees them.

JESUS came to set the captives free. What's holding you? What have you stuck? What is keeping you from moving forward? When you give it over to the Lord, where it happened, when it happened, how it happened will no longer matter. Those details will no longer be able to hold you captive or as a victim because you will no longer stay where you are. You will no longer be held prisoner. Come to JESUS! He's waiting. It does not matter how successful you are or how successful you have been, what you are going through (anger, frustration, hurt, helplessness, etc.). All of those feelings will not go away until you release it to the only ONE that can help you.

Luke 4:18-19 *(The VOICE) – The Spirit of the Lord the Eternal One is on Me. Why? Because the Eternal designated Me to be His representative to the poor, to preach good news to them. He sent Me to tell those who are held captive that they can now be set free, and to tell the blind that they can now see. He sent Me to liberate those held down by oppression. 19 In short, the Spirit is upon Me to proclaim that now is the time; this is the jubilee season of the Eternal One's grace.*

No matter where you have been in life, where you are in this life, why not make this year, this time, right now, be the year that you rise above every obstacle, hurt, disappointment, or frustrating and hopeless moment? Make this your time to shine. Let JESUS be your representative. Let Jesus be your healer.

There are times when we have prayed but do not see an immediate manifestation, and we tend to think that God either did not hear us or that His answer is "no." Have you ever heard the phrase, "delayed not denied?" Sometimes prayers get delayed in the spiritual realm. For example, look at Daniel, who was highly skilled in interpreting visions. He had a vision that not only did he not understand in its entirety but some of the vision made him very sick. Daniel prayed and fasted for three weeks. Finally, Gabriel the messenger angel told Daniel that God heard his prayer when he first prayed but the Prince of Persia had fought and held Gabriel up in the spiritual realm. Gabriel goes on to explain to Daniel that Michael the warring angel had to come and fight and help Gabriel get to Daniel with the message from God. The first thing that Gabriel said to Daniel is "Get up from there." We, too, can take that advice for whatever unpleasant situation that we have had to face. We need to get up from that place for God has heard us. Trust that He is working it out for us.

> ***1 John 5:14*** *– And this is the confidence that we have in him, that, if we ask any thing according to his will, he heareth us.*

If we do not know what God's will is for our life, ask Him and He will steer us in the right direction. Know that we have not because we ask not. Sometimes people are afraid to ask God for what they need because they think that God does not hear them or that God doesn't care. This is the furthest thing from the truth.

I know this personally. I was going through a very difficult time many years ago at a church I previously attended. A young teenage boy in the same church was also going through some difficult things with his parents. I do not know the extent of what he was going through or what really happened, but I know he and I shared similar issues.

He told me that he was homeless. The maternal part of me, my humanity, kicked in and I allowed him to spend nights over my house. Later on, I would allow his girlfriend to spend nights at my house as well. I had a four-bedroom house and would put them in different rooms. However, when I started to see things that were not quite right with this young man and I pointed them out to him, I noticed that he would become angry and indifferent.

Although we attended the same church, I had to remove myself from him. But before I totally removed myself from him, I took him to our pastor and told the pastor about him being somewhat homeless and that he needed help. I left it at that.

Eventually my relationships at the church became strained. There were a lot of accusations and negative comments made to me indirectly through the pastor. I was never confronted with what really happened. I knew is that I was being attacked over and from the pulpit. I eventually left but I did not want to. Somehow I thought that things would change and that the truth would come out. In the midst of everything, the Lord ushered me right out of that church. He came to me three times in my spirit.

The FIRST time God speaks...

The first time I was getting ready to be the Mistress of Ceremony at our church and I was down in the lady's room freshening up when my strand of pearls that I was wearing broke. I got some tissue and began to pick up the pearls on the floor. At that moment, the Spirit of the Lord spoke to my spirit and said, "Do not cast your pearls to a swine because he will trample them." I was stunned. I slowly went upstairs knowing that I was to be the M.C. of the program. I did it with no problem. Of course, I did not heed this first warning.

The SECOND time Gods speaks...

Another time the Lord spoke to my spirit and said to shake the dust off my feet. Again, I did not listen to or receive the voice of God because surely that is my voice talking to me, or so I thought. Although I knew the voice of God, when God's voice isn't saying what we want to hear, we will put what we know God is telling us on the backburner. I kept going. I kept teaching Sunday School. I kept preaching, but realized something wasn't right.

In the midst of the accusation, the persecution, and the trials, God gave me an open vision where the Lord showed and told me some things. What He told me resonated with me, even until this day. God first showed me a huge, black spider on my ceiling and its spider web. This spider was so big and black and the spider web was thick like a big two-stranded rope. God told me in this vision that someone was setting a trap for me. He said that I should fret not for I would not get in the trap. I previously asked God, "Do You care anything about what I was going through?" I asked the Lord this because I was going through some issues on my job, in my church, and even in my home. It felt like I was being ambushed on every side.

God sent a prophetess to the church that I was attending at the time. He didn't send just any ole prophet (not that a prophet or prophetess of God is just any ole body). He sent a well-known prophetess that used to be on the radio and was known as the singing prophet. The prophetess is sitting in the pulpit. I am sitting down on the floor on the first row. I'm watching God's prophetess. She looks around the room intently. Then she looks at me and nods her head. I wondered what her nod meant, but I would soon find out.

When it was time for her to minister, she came down on the floor and she came to me instantaneously. She began to prophesy many things to me. I remembered that she prophesied to me for a very long time. As the woman of God finished prophesying to me and began to walk back to the pulpit, she turned back and said, "God said that He cares about the smallest detail of your life. OH yeah, and concerning that trap, God said that He has your back." I briefly looked up into the pulpit at my then pastor who put his hand over his mouth and appeared to slide down in their chair.

I felt totally vindicated. Even though I never shared the entire story of what happened with anyone in the church, I did tell a close friend of mine at the church about the open vision that the Lord had showed me. Of course, it amazed her when the Prophetess talked about the spider web trap.

Did knowing that a trap was being set for me hurt me? Yes! Did the trap work? No! How could it? God had my back. *If God be for you, who can be against you* (Romans 8:31). They can try, but it will not work.

The THIRD time God speaks...

The Lord spoke to my spirit one final time concerning leaving my church, which I loved and did not want to leave. I was at Bible Study. The Pastor was teaching the Bible Study, but the Pastor is saying some things that I had shared in confidence. I am hurt and getting angry. I am sitting in the pew in the first or second row. I remember the pastor hovering over me.

All I could hear was silence. I do believe that the pastor was still speaking, but I could no longer hear what was being said. I remember turning my Bible to *James 16:1 these things have I spoken unto you, that ye should not be offended.* What things could the Lord be referring to? Don't cast your pearls? Shake the dust? And the Lord did not want me to be offended either. Wow! He knew at that point in time that being offended would be useless.

The Bible lets us know that offenses are going to come, but it's up to us to know what to do with those offenses. Those offenses are coming, and they may even come from the church.

I hear people saying that some things ought not to be in the church. I disagree. There are some things that have to happen in the church. Remember the Bible says, *let the wheat and the tare grow together and that God would do the separating* (Matthew 13:30). It is said that the tare and wheat looks very similar in nature and that you cannot uproot the tare because you will uproot the wheat, too. I strongly believe that when issues arise in the church, they should be addressed and properly dealt with in the church.

James 16:2 *– They shall put you out of the synagogues: yea, the time cometh, that whosoever killeth you will think that he doeth God service. 3 And these things will they do unto you, because they have not known the Father, nor me.*

God, what are you saying? Am I about to get kicked out of the church? More importantly, they don't know you. Then what is all this for? I mean the church, the preaching, the teaching, the time, the effort, and money. I could hear Arnold on the popular television show saying, "What you talkin' about Willis." But all jokes aside, I continued to read: *James 16:4 But these things have I told you, that when the time shall come, ye may remember that I told you of them. And these things I said not unto you at the beginning, because I was with you.*

I know that Jesus was talking to the disciples. He explained to them that He would be going away, but doesn't God speak to us through the Bible today? Isn't He with us in a special way, just as he was with the disciples? No matter how much I love the church and the people inside the church, if the Lord is constantly telling me that I have to go, then I must leave at once. That was it. I was not turning back or going back. I was moving straight ahead. Although I didn't get kicked out of the church, which I never knew them to throw anybody out of the church; I do believe if I had stayed that I would have gotten kicked out of the church.

A few years later, I heard the church did literally pick a lady up and put her outside of the church and lock the doors. I wonder how she is doing. She too should probably write a book.

WHO DID IT? AND HOW DID IT HAPPEN?

Events happen or things are said that cause hurt or pain so deep that you might not even want to talk about it. You might not know how to express it. That thing that happened, that caused you to be broken. I know for me that "thing" was a divorce. For someone else, it could have been child abuse, molestation by someone who was supposed to take care of you, but instead decided to allow their selfish nature to take advantage of you. Did a loved one die suddenly? Did a loved one suffer before they died with a long drawn out illness? Did someone promise you something in your church, on your job, in your home, but did not deliver? Did you realize the hard way that you were lied to? Did your father or mother get a divorce or separate and they failed to tell you that things were not working out? You heard the yelling, screaming, and fighting. One day when you came home from school, all the furniture was gone. Your father is sitting in a chair, in the middle of the room, crying because your mother moved on. In the alternative, your mother was there in the home and she did her best as your mother, but somehow it wasn't enough. As another scenario, your father was in the home, but he was too busy working or doing other things that appeared to be more important than taking care of and loving you. Was it a best friend that you trusted your deepest secrets with that betrayed you?

At some time in your life, it happened. You got hurt so bad and so deeply that you just didn't know what to do with all the pain and the hurt, which began to fester like meat marinating in a sauce. This hurt and pain marinated inside of you so long that it began to paralyze you. This was the devil's plan from the beginning. He knew if he could put you in bondage and keep you from moving forward, you would not fulfill your God-given destiny.

Although the Lord has helped us, there are some things we must do for ourselves in order to move forward. We must first trust God with everything inside of us. I know that some trust in houses. Some put their trust in their cars, their careers, their spouses. No. God wants us to put our total trust in Him. I know the situation is saying one thing and our feelings are saying another, but what is the Word of God saying? When we are in doubt, do not be afraid to pull the Bible out and ask God to speak to us through His Word.

Proverbs 3:5-6 – *Trust in the Lord with all thine heart; and lean not unto thine own* *understanding. In all thy ways acknowledge Him, and He shall direct thy paths.*

If we find ourselves in situations where we don't know what to do or where to go, we need to get down on our knees or lay prostrate before the Lord and ask Him. Listen to what that voice, His voice, is saying to us. If we listen intently, God will speak to us. He will speak to our heart. He will speak to our spirit for we were created in His likeness.

We are more spiritual than we really understand. That is how we know not to go to certain places. We might have been getting ready to go out to party or to hang out with some friends when we were younger, but we got this feeling deep down inside to not go. That is God leading us in the path of righteousness for His namesake. God can only lead us in the path of righteousness if we heed. ***If we heed, we can succeed***. I like that!

Life happens to all of us. We plan to do this and that, but right in the middle of our plans, something happens outside of our plans, and we find that life has derailed us. It is okay to cry because Jesus cried in the Garden of Gethsemane. He too wanted to know if this cup could pass.

We all have a cup and a cross that we **_must_** bear; a cup that we must drink from and, at other times, a cross that we must carry. Depression will try to creep in to make us feel sorry for ourselves or feel like a victim if we're not careful. Know that we are NOT victims, but we are the victors! We are winners. We are champions. God created us to be the winners that we are.

The very fact that you are reading this right now lets me know that we are on the winning side. God never told us that it would be easy. He never told us that the sun will shine every day, but He did tell us that *all things will work together for our good* (Romans 8:28). He did tell us that *no weapon formed against us shall prosper* (Isaiah 54:17).

What I love about God is that He loved and cared so much for us that He did warn us about the weapons that would form. He even told us to *be as wise as a serpent but harmless as a dove* (Matthew 10:16). He told us to *guard our hearts* (Proverbs 4:23). He told us how and why we must guard our hearts.

First, the Bible let us know why we must guard our heart in *Proverbs 4:23 Keep thy heart with all diligence; for out of it are the issues of life.* What are the issues? Things that matter the most to us we are holding in our heart. We hold these issues of life in our heart, whether they be good or bad. Therefore we must be careful of what we are holding in our hearts. Keep the good things. Let go of the bad things.

That's the why but here comes the how: *Ephesians 6:16, above all, taking the shield of faith, wherewith ye shall be able to quench all the fiery darts of the wicked.*

We must believe God, especially when we cannot see our way. The believers *walk by faith and not by sight* (2 Corinthians 5:7). Again, *faith is the substance of things hope for, evidence of things not seen* (Hebrews 11:1). We must believe God for the unthinkable and for the unbelievable.

God's ways are truly not our ways (Isaiah 55:8). I cannot begin to tell you how many jams God got me out of and how much red tape God helped me get through, knowing that had it not been for God, I would not have made it this far. The odds were stacked against me, like the odds that are stacked against some of you, too.

My mother and father both passed away 11 months apart of each other when I was only 18 and 19 years of age. Talk about the odds being against me. Of course I was hurt, deeply saddened that the two people who brought me into this life, raised me, fed me and loved me were gone in the blink of an eye.

Even when life rains on our parade, God can use that rain to sprout something good on the inside of us. God can cause strength to grow inside us and to help us persevere. God can give us peace in the midst of the storm. God can give us wisdom, but we have to know Him and trust Him that this peace, this strength, and this wisdom can be ours.

It is very important to know how and when to turn something over to the Lord. I say the faster, the better. Sometimes we tend to hold onto things a little longer than we should because we just do not know how to get rid of it. Think about spring-cleaning. That is a time that we are not only going to clean those hard to get to places inside and outside the home, but it is also a time when we pack unwanted things and donate them to various organizations. Doesn't one also do spring cleaning for the soul?

One reason why we are reluctant to spring clean (totally removing all unwanted and unneeded items from our lives) is that we hold on to hurt and anger too long because we feel we have a right to be angry or we have a right to be hurt. We need to recognize that this reluctance and feelings are another plan from satan to keep us in bondage so that we will abort and forfeit our God-given destiny.

That is why it is important to forgive people. Sometimes people are unaware of the hurt that they have placed upon you. Other times they really do not care about what they have done to you. However, you have the choice to forgive. Forgive them anyhow. Let God deal with them. This does not mean you must hang out with them or go to lunch or dinner with them. It means that you must forgive them. *Do yourself a favor and forgive them.*

And I'll give you a little help right here. Always remember that God is the judge. God told us to forgive and that He's the judge. Trust that God will handle the situation. Remember, that no matter what, God LOVES you and can right every wrong. Live your life while God is working behind the scenes.

One more thing to remember is that we are only forgiven as much as we forgive. Be honest and admit that we may have may have been the offender at one time as well. We would not want someone to hold unforgiveness over our heads. We *owe no man nothing but to love them* (Romans 13:8).

Do you know that some people have died from a broken heart because they just did not know how to process the pain and let it go? The event did happen. The pain was real, but to abort your mission on Earth was not God's plan for your life. You must trust God to see past what has and is currently happening. It could be happening right now, but trust God to see what the end is going to be. God told Jeremiah *I know the thoughts that I think towards you to prosper you and give you expected end* (Jeremiah 29:11).

Jeremiah was a teenager when God called him to greatness. He was *called from your mother's womb* to greatness (Jeremiah 1:11). You too may be called to greatness, but might not know it until you became a teenager or an adult. The sooner you find out this important information, the faster you can begin achieving your God-given goals.

This chapter started with the questions, "Who did it?" and "How did it happen? Whatever the "it" is, "it" has already happened. So, why are you allowing something that cannot change to continue to hold you back? Acknowledge that it happened and the pain is real, but give that pain to the **ONLY ONE** who could carry such a load. We need the peace. We need the rest. We need our freedom to move on. We have been carrying this bad stuff around way too long. We must pray, bind up some things, take our God-given authority on the Earth, read the Word of God, and let the Word, instead of the worry, marinate within our souls. Watch us become stronger, wiser, and better people. What was meant to hinder us will now become our stepping-stone.

And I know that all things work together for the good of them that love the Lord and is the called according to His purpose (Romans 8:38). Think about the many people that we have helped or are going to help with our story, including the ones who hurt us the most. The bad stuff will not just work out for us, but the bad stuff, when we learn from it, grow from, and get free of it, will be used to help someone else.

I remember many years ago, my pastor came to me and asked me to counsel this young lady. The pastor asked me because no one on the ministerial staff had ever had this happen in their marriage and/or their life, including the pastor. I agreed to counsel the young lady, but I must admit, my first thought was, "seriously Lord? I am the ONLY one out of about 13-15 ministers (including the pastor) who has NEVER been through something like this before?" At first, I did not know how to feel about the request, but upon counseling the young lady, I focused quickly and precisely on a few key issues. I could see the immediate relief and joy that the young lady experienced right there in that moment. I believe it was at that moment that I realized a lot of what happened to us in this life is not just for us, but is to help someone else as well.

> *1 Thessalonians 5:11* – *Wherefore comfort yourselves together, and edify one another, even as also ye do.*

When we encourage, counsel, or edify a person, we are building that person up where life has torn them down. We are building them up to be better, stronger, and wiser than before. Then, they too can help somebody else.

Think about it. It's just like a doctor or lawyer that has studied to help someone to become better or to stay free. We are working undercover as an agent for the Lord to help somebody become better or to deliver them out of whatever bondage that is or was holding them.

There are three things to remember when we are hurting and do not know what to do:

1) God will never leave us or forsake us. God is always there.

2) This too shall pass. It will not always be (feel) like this.

3) We will make it through the tough (dark) times.

Remember, no matter what we encounter in this life, we already have the victory. One might think how can I have victory in death? Christians, Believers, Children of God are *more than a conqueror* (Romans 8:37). We can win battles, but only when we win the war can we say that we have the victory and because our victory comes from God alone, we confidently declare that we have the victory even when the sun is not shining so bright in our lives.

> **Romans 8:37** – Nay, in all these things we are more than conquerors through him that loved us.

Death cannot defeat us. The grave cannot hold us.

> **1 Corinthians 15:55** – O death, where is thy sting? O grave, where is thy victory? ⁵⁶ The sting of death is sin; and the strength of sin is the law. ⁵⁷ But thanks be to God, which giveth us the victory through our Lord Jesus Christ.

In other words, death gets its power to hurt us from the sin or sins that we commit. Sin gets its power from the Law, but God is the one who gives us victory through Jesus, who was crucified on Calvary's cross. I just want to pause to say, "THANK YOU, Lord."

COPING WITH LOSS

When a person goes through divorce, it is very difficult for many reasons. I believe one of the hardest things to cope with in a divorce is when the marriage ends and the marital grieving process occurs. Divorce is like death. It is difficult because we know that we will grieve when we lose a loved one that has transitioned. It is difficult when something that has been promised to you has ended; yet the person is still alive, breathing, and walking. When you are a Christian, there is an added stigma that comes along with a marriage that has ended in divorce because the Bible strongly speaks against divorce. If you are not careful, you may feel depressed and like a failure. One good thing that we as Christians know is that there is no failure in Christ Jesus.

Even if a marriage fails, this does not make you a failure or mean that you have done something wrong to cause the breakdown or the dissolution of the marriage. Because there is no failure in Christ, and if Christ is in you, then there is no failure in you. You may make mistakes, but the good thing about most mistakes is that you have the opportunity to learn from your mistake(s).

Realize that you must separate you "the person" from the failed marriage "the situation."

Let's be honest, I believe that in most marriages, there is something that we ALL can learn. There are things that we can do better and maybe even differently. We learn from what did not or what does not work so that in the future you will not make the same mistake(s) again.

The Bible strongly speaks against divorce. Malachi lets us know that God hates divorce.

***Malachi 2:16** (VOICE) – Eternal One: For I, the God of Israel, hate divorce! The Bible clearly tells us just as in the days of Noah that people will be marrying and giving into marriage.*

Jesus even had a side session to explain how the Father does not like divorce. As Christians, when we go through something as traumatic as a divorce, we not only have to go through the grieving process, but we have to grasp the concept that although God hates divorce, He still loves the divorcee. God knows that divorce breaks a person spiritually, mentally, emotionally and physically. In the Old Testament, the reason why God approved divorce is because the husband was the sole provider, and if the husband's heart became hardened against his wife, the husband would not provide for the wife, which meant that the wife could lack having food to eat or even shelter.

Although I have been divorced more than once, when I counsel couples, I ask the couple what are their deal breakers in the marriage. They began to rattle off things like adultery, lying, etc. I stop them and let them know that they should never go into a marriage with deal breakers. However, you should go into the marriage knowing that there is going to be work that must be done. We look at fairytales on the television. We read fairytales in books. When your marriage falls short of what you read and what you saw on television, you feel like you have been tricked and trapped.

I do not like to hear people say that they outgrew one another. You outgrow clothes. You outgrow shoes. You outgrow music, but you do not outgrow marriages. You are supposed to grow together and accept each other for who they are. We have to learn how to forgive. We have to learn how to love the way that God says that we are to love. I believe that some marriages do not succeed because there is not enough love and not enough effort (work) put into the relationship. I also let couples know that God hates divorce so they really need to consider if this is something that they truly want to do.

> ***Matthew 24: 37 –*** *But as the days of Noah were, so shall also the coming of the Son of man be.38 For as in the days that were before the flood they were eating and drinking, marrying and giving in marriage, until the day that Noe entered into the ark...*

We must look at what was really happening in the days of Noah to compare them current day. However, that would be another book. What I would like to point out is that perhaps they were getting married and getting divorced in Noah's day too, which would suggest that the nature of man (and woman) may have become self-indulging and selfish, thinking more about oneself than others. In a marriage, we must be selfless, caring, and giving. You have to give even if you don't feel like it. You give because you know that it is the right thing to do. Anything worth having is worth fighting for.

Also, what this strongly suggests is that in the day of Noah is that just as there was no real commitment to God through the people back then and that there is no real commitment to God by many people today, there is a lack of commitment in marriage and to the sanctity of marriage. Of course, this does not hold true for all people.

If we were committed to God the way that we are supposed to be, I believe we would be more tolerant of each others' shortcomings. We will not just end a marriage because we say it is too hard, or we don't want to talk about it, or that it is too much work. In my case, that is exactly what I was told by my now ex-husband. The judge summed it up when my divorce was granted right on the spot on the grounds of "mental cruelty"

Broken Beyond Belief

When I think about loss, I tend to think about Mephibosheth in the Bible (2 Samuel 9). Mephibosheth was the grandson of King Saul. Mephibosheth was royalty, living in a palace until his father, Jonathan, and his grandfather, King Saul, got killed in battle. When the nurse heard this, she picked up Mephibosheth and tried to run with him, to get Mephibosheth to a safe place. In the midst of everything, she dropped Mephibosheth and he landed on both of his feet, crippling him.

Mephibosheth was five years of age when this happened. Mephibosheth was unable to go back to the king's palace. He was hidden and raised in Lodebar. Lodebar is a Hebrew word that means a place of lack. It is my belief that Mephibosheth barely had shelter and just enough to eat. Maybe, Lodebar was like a run-downed place with condemned buildings and vacant lots. What I like about this story is that when David got in a place that he could help Mephibosheth, David went back and asked, "Is there anybody left in the house of Saul that I can show kindness to?"

The people told David that Mephibosheth was in Lodebar. When Mephibosheth came into the presence of

David, Mephibosheth referred to himself as a "dead dog." I like to point this out because I do not feel like Mephibosheth was in a "woe is me state", but I feel like Mephibosheth had been in a place of lack in his life for a very long time and accepted where he was and that he did not expect change to come his way.

Not only did God bring him out of a place of lack, God brought Mephibosheth to the king's palace. In doing so, God blessed all of his servants in the midst of blessing Mephibosheth. God brought Mephibosheth from the pit to the palace. Some of your own family and friends are blessed because of you. God is not a respecter of person, but God does show favor upon certain individuals that trust and believe in Him.

> ***2 Samuel 9:7-9*** *– And David said unto him, Fear not: for I will surely shew thee kindness for Jonathan thy father's sake, and will restore thee all the land of Saul thy father; and thou shalt eat bread at my table continually. ⁸ And he bowed himself, and said, What is thy servant, that thou shouldest look upon such a dead dog as I*

am? *⁹ Then the king called to Ziba, Saul's servant, and said unto him, I have given unto thy master's son all that pertained to Saul and to all his house.*

Mephibosheth suffered great losses, one after the other. His grandfather and his father died in battle on the same day, and he would become crippled in that very hour, but God did not forget Mephibosheth. God restored all of the material things that he lost and even brought Mephibosheth back to the palace.

When you divorce, you may have to deal with great losses. You may have to lose things, like a house, car, and dog. Losses may be greater if there are children involved. However, God knows how to restore everything back to you on His timing.

Another great passage in the Bible that talks about God's restoration and provision is from the Book of Job. Job lost all of his children and his cattle. Job had four friends that tried to encourage Job. His friends were trying to encourage him because Job's friends did at least three things right that as evidenced in Job 2:11–13.

FIRST, they came to Job when he was suffering. SECOND, they empathized with him: *"they began to weep aloud, and they tore their robes and sprinkled dust on their heads"* (verse 12). THIRD, they spent time with him.

Verse 13 states they were with him for seven days before they offered their advice. They expressed their sympathy for Job by sitting with Job in silence. They did not immediately talk, therefore, they did not immediately begin to accuse Job of doing something wrong, but when they began to speak, they accused Job of doing something wrong.

The LORD did allow satan to attack Job's health, family, and finances. However, it doesn't end there. When it was all said and done, God gave Job back everything that he had lost and then some. That, my friend, is called OVERFLOW! God blessed Job beyond what one could measure. Although God blessed Job with more children, I am sure that God healed the hurt that only a mother or father could know when they suffer a great loss, such as losing a child.

When you deal with loss, you deal with something that you once had, but you no longer have. We have to remember that we have an enemy named satan. As satan was looking for someone to devour in the Book of Job, satan has a mission and his mission is to kill, steal, and destroy. What I love about God is that God asked satan if he had tested and tried His faithful servant Job because Job had done something right, not wrong.

At times, God uses us as trophies. We do not know what is going on behind the scene as there are things that occur in the spirit realm that we know nothing about. This is the reason why it is so important for us to trust God.

> ***John 10:10*** *– The thief cometh not, but for to steal, and to kill, and to destroy: I am come that they might have life, and that they might have it more abundantly.*

satan comes to steal, but God comes to heal. When you have God in your life, then you know that your story does not end in pain.

satan's objective is stated in John 10:10, where satan is referred to as a thief. satan would love to not only steal, kill, or destroy, but also steal peace, joy, and one's soul. God tells us in His word to not fear those who can kill the body, but fear the one that holds your life in the palm of His hand (Matthew 10:28). That person is God himself. The fear God is referring to is not a fear of being scared, but a respect and honor. We should have such a love and respect for God that we should not allow anyone or anything to interfere with that relationship, not even death.

***Matthew 10:28** – And fear not them which kill the body, but are not able to kill the soul: but rather fear him which is able to destroy both soul and body in hell.*

The Apostle Paul was so convinced of this when he stated the following in Romans 8: 35*Who shall separate us from the love of Christ? shall tribulation, or distress, or persecution, or famine, or nakedness, or peril, or sword?* 36 *As it is written, For thy sake we are killed all the day long; we are accounted as sheep for the slaughter.* 37 *Nay, in all these things we are more than conquerors through him that loved us.* 38 *For I am persuaded, that neither* *death, nor life, nor angels, nor principalities, nor powers, nor things present, nor things to come, 39 Nor height, nor depth, nor any other creature, shall be able to separate us from the love of God, which is in Christ Jesus our Lord.*

People think if they end their life, they end all of their problems. That is furthest from the truth. I do sympathize and understand that a person can be in such a broken state that they feel that there is no way out. However, no matter what the problem is or how bad things seem, it is important to understand that God is Omniscient. He is all knowing. He has <u>all</u> the answers, <u>all</u> the time. It is important that we rely on God at <u>all</u> times and give God an opportunity to change things in our lives, turning things around.

That thing that is bringing you grief today can be the same thing that can bring you joy tomorrow. Think about it. There are people who may cry that I had to walk away from three babies that I loved dearly; or I had to take my car back to the dealership; or I had to live in "Lodebar", which is current day Cabrini Green for me.

In my case, I was thankful for shelter and grateful to be able to spend time around a lot of my relatives. I later found myself without employment. Even in all of my losses, God kept blessing me one by one. He blessed me to get another car and I paid cash for the car. No car note!

I eventually got another job. I was able to rent an apartment in the suburbs of Chicago. My son eventually came to live with me, which was a great help because he helped me with some of the bills. God kept right on blessing me. I became engaged and later got married. God didn't just give me anybody. God gave me a man of God, who would love me for me and adore me. I adore him right back.

My husband asked me if I like bowling. I LOVE bowling. My son was on a bowling league, winning two trophies, including one first-place trophy. Eventually, my son quit bowling because he told me that bowling was my passion and not his. To this day, my son will occasionally bowl with the family for fun. So, my husband asked me if I wanted to go bowling. I go bowling. What I did not know is that it was a date.

My sister was the one that pointed that out to me. She said that she wrote in her journal, "Thank you, Lord, for allowing my sister to go on a date."

I told my sister that it was not a date. She said, "Yes, it was. Ask him."

I called my now husband and asked him if that was a date because my sister seems to think that it was. He said that he knew it was a date when he asked me to go bowling.

Wow! I was kind of sheltered growing up. We began to court. We courted for a long time because he understood that I had just came out of a broken marriage and he wanted to give me time. In all fairness, my husband had a couple of failed marriages too so we really understood each other.

During our "courting" period, we went on many picnics in the park, bowling dates, dinner dates, and bike rides. We talked a lot. In his own way, he would ask me lots of questions about my failed marriages. I knew what he was doing. He was counseling me. He was so smart and careful in the way he would approach each subject.

I think that I am falling for this guy. Even now, we enjoy so many of the same things. Currently, we both work hard in the ministry together at our church. We love most of the same movies and food. It's amazing! I am grateful to

God for healing me and allowing me to move forward to meet someone similar to myself.

What if I had ended my story in despair? Always give God a chance to work things out in your life. Even if we are the ones that make the mistake(s). Sometimes your parents or your family and friends may tell you not to marry a person. You marry that person anyway. The marriage ends in divorce. Yet, know that you followed your heart, rather than your mind. You must forgive yourself and know that God forgives you too.

Allow yourself to make mistakes. Allow yourself to grow from your mistakes, but do not get stuck in your mistake(s). One thing about being broken is that you do not have to stay broken. God is the Potter. We are truly the clay that the Potter wants to put back together again.

It saddens my heart when I hear people that have experienced divorce and truly desire to be married again, but think that God will not grant them another chance at marriage because they have been divorced. Are you serious? No. God loves you and wants the best for you.

I like what the Apostle Paul said in Philippians 4:12 *I know both how to be abased, and I know how to abound: everywhere and in all things I am instructed both to be full and to be hungry, both to abound and to suffer need.* Paul was simply saying that there were times in his life when he had an overflow, an abundance, and more than enough money, love, shelter, etc. There were other times in his life when he either didn't have any or not enough. But, Paul said that he learned how to be content in every situation.

This peace that Paul came to know was achieved through his trials, tribulations, and relationship with the Lord. In the Bible, we learn that Paul had been shipwrecked three times and God spared his life each time. Paul was almost stoned to death. God again spared Paul's life. Amongst other things, Paul had been beaten and imprisoned. Most people would have given up but, no matter how bad his situation, Paul recognized God's provisions in his life. Paul said it best in Philippians 4:19 *But my God shall supply all your need according to his riches in glory by Christ Jesus.*

The peace that Paul had was due to Jesus. The Bible often times referred to Jesus as Peace. If Paul could allow

Jesus to be his peace and I can allow Jesus to be my peace, why can't you allow Jesus to bring you and be your peace, too? The older saints used to sing a song, "Have you tried Jesus, He's alright." Well, Jesus is better than alright.

> ***Isaiah 9:6*** *– For unto us a child is born, unto us a son is given: and the government shall be upon his shoulder: and his name shall be called Wonderful, Counsellor, The mighty God, The everlasting Father, The Prince of Peace.*

Not only do we recognize that Jesus is our Peace, but Jesus is the leader of Peace. Notice that whenever Jesus is referred to as Peace in the Bible, the word "Peace" is often capitalized.

> ***Luke 24:36*** *– And as they thus spake, Jesus himself stood in the midst of them, and saith unto them, Peace be unto you.*

Each scripture about "Peace" that Jesus refers to deals with different situations and scenarios. In one story, Jesus and the disciples were traveling in a boat.

__Mark 4:39__ – And He arose, and rebuked the wind, and said unto the sea, Peace, be still. And the wind ceased, and there was a great calm.

A bad storm had arisen and Jesus slept through the storm. The disciples woke Jesus and asked Him if he cared about them. The disciples asked this question for a few reasons. First, they thought that the storm was going to overtake the boat and they would drown, losing their lives. Second, the disciples were fearful because they lacked faith. Jesus is the Captain and He commands Peace, stillness, and calmness.

Although the disciples were afraid of the storm, like we become afraid of the storms that rise in our lives, Jesus was not afraid. When Jesus arose, He rose with confidence. He rose with assurance and speaking the Word, such that the storm calmed. Why don't you let Jesus rise in your current situation? My situation may have been a failed marriage, but you may be suffering some another type of loss. Make Jesus bigger than your circumstances today.

Peace isn't something that we just want. Peace is something that we all need in our lives to function as healthy and whole individuals. In the Old Testament, people sacrificed various animals to God for , but because Jesus is our Savior, we do not have to go through those formalities any longer to come into God's presence or to obtain God's peace. One thing we must remember is that we do have an enemy that comes to kill, steal, and destroy. The enemy doesn't try to take just material things away from us, but tries to take from us personal things and relationships that matter the most. Maybe, that is why people that cause us the most hurt in our lives are the people that are closest to us. In many cases, this could be the people in your own home, on your job, or in the church. It is the people that we have to interact with the most. That is what I love about Jesus. He provided us with Peace through the storms of our lives. We don't have to wait until that storm is over to have Peace. Hallelujah!

John 14:27 *– Peace I leave with you, my peace I give unto you: not as the world giveth, give I unto you. Let not your heart be troubled, neither let it be afraid.*

Jesus' peace is not based on conditions in the world. It is not based on whether something good or bad is happening in our lives, but this peace is the confidence that we have that Christ knows that no matter what we have to go through in this life, we can be assured that everything is going to be okay one way or another even before seeing the end results.

Philippians 4:6-7 *– Be careful for nothing; but in everything by prayer and supplication with thanksgiving let your requests be made known unto God. 7And the peace of God, which passeth all understanding, shall keep your hearts and minds through Christ Jesus.*

Although the peace of God cannot always be understood by man, we must remember not to fret or worry. We must pray to the Lord in every situation, If there is something we do not understand, we must ask God and always remember to be appreciative, knowing that God is faithful and concerned about everything that concerns us.

> ***Colossians 3:15*** *– And let the peace of God rule in your hearts, to which also ye are called in one body; and be ye thankful.*

In this passage, Paul tells us to "let the peace of God rule in your hearts." Our heart is where we feel everything good or bad. Our secret desires, thoughts, and jealousies are in our heart. If we allow the Lord to rule our hearts with His peace, then and only then will we be able to work well together in the church, in our homes, and even on our jobs. Let's not forget our communities.

One thing I can remember as a child is how my father would make me speak to everybody, even people that

I did not like, I never understood why he would make me do such a thing. I would ask my father, "Why do I have to speak to her?" My father would always reply "It doesn't cost you anything to speak to a person." Now, I wish that we were more like that today, but I noticed that most people do not speak. Now, I just try to give a polite smile and nod. Oh, how I wish we could get back to the old days of speaking to each other and greeting others with "hello" or "hi."

In going through this life, we sometimes lose things that are dear to us but remember that people come and go in our lives for many reasons. Everything that happens in our lives is seasonal. Change will come to our lives because nothing remains the same. Know that because we accept Jesus, we can cope with loss or anything that comes.

COPING WITH BROKEN PROMISES

A vow is a sincere promise that should not be taken lightly. When we make a vow, we take an oath or a pledge to do something. Look at what happens during the exchange of vows at a wedding. We promise to be committed to that person no matter what we go through. We promise to be dedicated through the good times as well as the difficult times.

> ***Deuteronomy 23:21, 23*** – *When thou shalt vow a vow unto the LORD thy God, thou shalt not slack to pay it: for the LORD thy God will surely require it of thee; and it would be sin in thee. 23 That which is gone out of thy lips thou shalt keep and perform; even a freewill offering, according as thou hast vowed unto the LORD thy God, which thou hast promised with thy mouth.*

When we make our marital vows, they should not be taken lightly. These vows should be made with honesty, sincerity, and with the best intentions. The first commitment belongs to God because God is the one who told us to be married. God, not man, implemented marriage. God understands the importance of being married more than people. After all, it was God who said that it is not good for man to be alone.

> **Genesis 2:18** - *And the LORD God said, It is not good that the man should be alone; I will make him an help meet for him.*

God understood that if the animals of the Earth needed companionship, man would need someone to communicate with, be intimate with, and that could help him to be the best that he could be.

Second, this commitment should be made to the person that we choose as our lifetime mate. The divorce rate is very high and even higher amongst the Christian community. According to The Huffington Post and The Gospel Coalition (TGC), there has been a breakdown in

Christian marriages. Such reports indicate that there is something very wrong with how we view marriages today.

> ***Matthew 24:38*** *For as in the days that were before the flood they were eating and drinking, marrying and giving in marriage, until the day that Noah entered into the ark;*

The Bible says that in the days of Noah, people will be eating, drinking, marrying, and giving into marriage which in my opinion means that people will be getting married and divorced. I believe that there is an overall lack of commitment to God. If you are not committed to God, it's impossible for you to be wholly committed to another human being. I also believe that some, not all, people have their priorities off especially when it comes to being married. Sometimes we get married thinking about what the other person can do for me; not so much what we can do for each other. Although, the wife is the help mate and the man is the provider, women are supposed to help their husband's do some things but if they are not doing anything, then we cannot fulfill our roles properly as wives. I think that our views and priorities have become distorted. Is there too much partying going on? Are we more focus on festivities today rather than the longevity of our commitment to each other?

When Hannah, Samuel's mom, made a vow to the Lord, it was sincere.

> ***1 Samuel 1:11*** *– And she vowed a vow, and said, O LORD of hosts, if thou wilt indeed look on the affliction of thine handmaid, and remember me, and not forget thine handmaid, but wilt give unto thine handmaid a man child, then I will give him unto the LORD all the days of his life, and there shall no razor come upon his head.*

It was very important to have a man-child. Hannah was barren therefore she was more than likely looked down upon by the other women in her family and in her hometown. The Lord not only granted Hannah to have

Samuel Hannah had a total of five children with a couple of girls mixed in there. When Hannah made her vow, she was sincere and she kept the promise that she had made to the Lord.

The Lord is the one that implemented marriage from the beginning between a man and a woman, with Adam and Eve being the first couple. When you begin to take marriage and make a mockery out of it, you really are making a fool of yourself because God already said in His word that He is God and that He cannot be mocked.

Marriage is a commitment, a promise and a vow that you make to God first and then to man. When we deviate from the plan and the will of God, that's when things become distorted and perverted. Anything that is the opposite of God's will is a perversion. Of course, today we deal with a lot of perversion, even in our own families. The world gets angry when we do not accept their rules but the world must realize anything opposite of God's plan is an exception to the rule and we as a Christian have the right to obey the Word of God in its entirety.

Anyone who has made the commitment to be married and then find themselves faced with being divorced must go through a grieving period, which the world may not recognize that is needed. Although it is shown that the divorce rate is on a decline, statistics shows that every 13 seconds that there is a divorce in America; that's 277 divorce per hour, 6,646 divorce per day, 46,523 divorce per week and 2,419,196 divorce per year (http://www.wf-lawyers.com/divorce-statistics-and-facts/). What I see from this report is that there are still over 2 million conceivably hurting people a year, who possibly do not know what to do after a divorce.

What we must understand is that not just women get divorce but men get divorce too and men experience the hurt and separation as well. Both men and women must know how to pick up the pieces in order to move on and find the closure that is needed. However, the most IMPORTANT thing to remember is that you do NOT have to pick up all the pieces at one time, it's a process we (divorcees) must go through.

I'm not saying that any of us are perfect because if we were, Jesus would not have had to die for our sins. Because we are imperfect human beings is the very reason why Jesus was made a sacrifice for us. The only difference between a Christian and a non-Christian is that we as Christians recognize our sins and we admit our faults and we recognize and accept Jesus as our personal Savior; in doing so, this helps us to become better and more mature people. God loves us so much, not only did He give us His only begotten Son, but He gave us grace and mercy too to help us along the way. What a mighty God we serve! That song comes to my mind right now, "angels bow before Him, Heaven and Earth adores Him, what a mighty God we serve." Amen and it is so.

In fact, every knee will bow acknowledging that Jesus is Lord. For many that will bow, it will be too late, but as long as we have breath in our bodies, it is never too late to make a change. I am totally convinced of this because Romans 1:18 said that *God has put the knowledge in all of our hearts to know who He is*; therefore on Judgment Day, we will be without excuse. Yes, we know Him, even that person who deliberately sins knows of God but that person just chooses not to follow the Lord. They're more interested in doing things that pleases their flesh rather than being committed to the things that pleases God. We know that we were made of flesh to begin with because of sin.

Anything that is broken needs to be fixed and that doesn't necessarily mean that every marriage that ends in divorce will be fixed but we must understand when a marriage becomes broken, so does that person, or in some cases both parties, become broken. When this happens, you need to be made whole again so that you can function in this society at your fullest and at your best. That broken marriage, those broken vows, and broken promises are just setbacks that need to be dealt with especially in the Christian community.

A broken marriage can leave one to feel a sense of personal failure. We as Christians know that there is no failure in Christ Jesus. It's impossible to accept Jesus as your personal Savior and be a failure so you must go through the process of grieving and in some cases, you might even experience anger but one must never become bitter, we must strive to become better. I mention bitter because bitterness is just hurt and anger mixed together that has never been dealt with.

Here is a list of things that you can do help your broken heart mend faster and can help you to become better instead of bitter:

I'M EMOTIONAL...

1. Be in touched with your emotions. If you're hurting, don't try to run from the pain, but instead embrace the pain. Accepting the pain allows you to begin the healing process sooner rather than later. Don't be afraid to pray to your Father in Heaven.

> ***Psalm 50:15*** *And call on me in the day of trouble: I will deliver you, and you shall glorify me.*

The Lord is waiting to help you. He wants to help you. He wants to deliver you from the hurt, He wants to deliver you from the pain, from the depression, the anger, etc., whatever is plaguing you; Daddy God wants to put a stop to it. He wants to heal you – He wants to make you whole. Once you're delivered, then you can have an awesome testimony of how you made it through. This will bring your Father in Heaven much glory.

Once you handle your emotions, your emotions will not be able to handle (overpower) you.

I'M ALONE…

2. Do not be afraid to be alone – allow yourself some alone time. Being alone at times allows you to be in touch with your emotions. When you're alone, this is a good time to pray, meditate and reflect. Praying will also build up your inner man and this will help you to gain your strength back faster as well. Remember, Paul said that when he was strong that he was weak and when he was weak that he was strong. Paul became stronger in his weakness because he allowed God to help strengthen him. Just cry out to your Father in Heaven so that He can help you.

I'M CRYING…

3. Cry as often as you need to and as loud as you want to. Everybody handle things differently and maybe you're not a crier and that's okay too but if you are a person who likes to shed a tear or two, do it. Why not? One of my friends said that tears are our muscles. The tears

help you to grow stronger and don't forget God bottle up our tears and not one of them will go to waste.

> ***Psalm 56:8*** *(VOICE) You have taken note of my journey through life, caught each of my tears in Your bottle. But God, are they not also blots on Your book?*

Not only does God bottle up our tears, but God has a book with our tears in it. Let your tears tell your story to God.

I'M NOT BLAMING YOU...

4. Don't just look at the other person fault(s); see if you could have done something differently. Anything that you can do differently or better can be used as a 'positive' in your next relationship. One thing I used to do is stay on the telephone entirely too much and too long. That time that you're using excessively to talk on the phone really takes away quality time from being with your family or your spouse. That is time that you cannot get back. I refused to carry that behavior into this relationship. Ephesians 5 lets us know that *we*

should redeem the time. Spend better use of my time and make it quality time. Yes, marriage is a ministry just in case you don't know that. Your spouse needs you as much as you may need your spouse.

I'M APOLOGIZING...

5. If you are the cause of the breakdown of the marriage, apologize and forgive yourself. The only way you will be able to remove the guilt is to handle the guilt head on. If you do not handle the guilt (the dirty deed that you did), then the guilt will turn into shame. Shame is a painful feeling of humiliation or distressed cause by your conscious mind replaying the event over and over in your mind. Why? Because you did not handle the guilt head on. Realize that you are human and that you are susceptible to making a mistake and even if your spouse or your ex does not forgive you, always know that God will forgive you.

> ***Psalm 4:1*** *Hear me when I call, O God of my righteousness: thou hast enlarged me*

> *when I was in distress; have mercy upon me, and hear my prayer.*

God will have mercy upon you, even if you're the offender. You just need to be sincere and invoke the help of the One that can truly help you.

I'M NOT HOLDING GRUDGES...

6. If you are not the cause of the breakdown of the marriage, do not hold grudges; forgive the other person even if they never say that they're sorry – life is too short to hold onto grudges and grudges can block your blessings. There is a saying, 'when you hold grudges, your hands are not free to catch blessings.' Therefore, you can't receive all that God has for you if you are not willing to release the other person. Remember that we're only forgiven by our Father as much as we forgive our offenders. God is so serious about this until He won't even accept our offerings at the altar. He said if you bring an offering to the altar and you remember that your brother has an ought against you, leave the offering at the altar and go to your brother and

reconcile. Even if the relationship does not come back together, at least agree to live apart peacefully.

I'M NOT REHEARSING BAD MEMORIES...

7. Don't constantly think, repeat or discuss the bad events. Yes, they happened and after you have confided in someone close to you, it's best to fill your thoughts with happy thoughts. Don't know what to think on...Philippians 4 tells us *"...whatsoever things are true, whatsoever things are honest, whatsoever things are just, whatsoever things are pure, whatsoever things are lovely, whatsoever things are of good report; if there be any virtue, and if there be any praise, think on these things."*

This will be a good time to meditate on the Word of God and learn some scriptures. Here are a few scriptures you can think on:

Philippians 4:13 *I can do ALL things through Christ which strengtheneth me.*

You can and you will get through this.

Romans 8:28 *And we know that all things work together for good to them that love God, to them who are the called according to his purpose.*

No matter how bad it feels or look, God know how to turn this around to bless you.

Isaiah 54:17 *No weapon that is formed against thee shall prosper; and every tongue that shall rise against thee in judgment thou shalt condemn. This is the heritage of the servants of the Lord, and their righteousness is of me, saith the Lord.*

I'm a fighter and although I understand that weapons will form. I, also, understand the weapons will not work.

Psalm 147:3 *He healeth the broken in heart, and bindeth up their wounds.*

We must focus on things that will help us to become better, as opposed to becoming bitter. We must always remember Romans 8:28... *And we know that all things work together for good to them that love God, to them who are the called according to his purpose.* No matter what it looks like, no matter how bad it hurts and even if we don't understand why this is happening, just always remember that everything will line up in your life the way that the Lord has ordained for it to be.

***Jonah 1:16** – Then the men feared the LORD exceedingly, and offered a sacrifice unto the LORD, and made vows.*

In the Old Testament, it was very common for the people to make all kinds of sacrifices to the LORD and generally these sacrifices came in the form of animals. Each animal represented a certain type of sacrifice. In this particular verse, fear meant respect, so the men respected the LORD so much that they offered a sacrifice and made a vow. I think we miss that as people when we make a vow, a sacrifice is definitely involved. I believe if you want to have a successful marriage, you must respect each other and know that because of the vow that you made, sacrifices must be made on a continuous basis.

From the time of Adam and Eve to the time of Jesus Christ, the Lord's people practiced the law of sacrifice. They were commanded to offer as sacrifices the firstlings of their flocks. These animals had to be perfect, without blemish. The command was given to remind the people that Jesus Christ, the Firstborn of the Father, would come into the world. He would be perfect in every way, and He would offer Himself as a sacrifice for our sins (Leviticus 4).

Sacrifice today means giving to the Lord whatever He requires of us, whether it's our time, our earthly possessions, and our energies to further His work. The Lord commanded, *"Seek ye first the kingdom of God, and his righteousness"* (Matthew 6:33). Our willingness to sacrifice is an indication of our devotion to God. People have always been tried and tested to see if they will put the things of God first in their lives.

The Apostle Paul even told us to *present our bodies a living sacrifice* (Romans 12:1). Paul said that this is our reasonable service. When you think about it, if God is Holy and He told us to be Holy, this only makes sense. Presenting our lives as a living sacrifice produces pain at the time, requires cutting away of the world's residue but presenting ourselves as a living sacrifice to the Lord puts us in the presence of God. Only through sacrifices can we obtain eternal life that Jesus offers to us.

We may not be asked to sacrifice all things. But like Abraham, we should be willing to sacrifice everything we have in our possession. Not that this makes us worthy to be in God's presence but it makes us trustworthy. God wants people that will be able to love, trust and obey Him. I'm not saying this is always easy but trusting, loving and obeying the Lord is something that we should work on daily.

Isaac was promised to Abraham and Sarah and for reasons unknown to man, God told Abraham to sacrifice Isaac. Wait a minute – wasn't Isaac the promise? Isn't marriage a promise but now your marriage lay on the altar to be sacrificed. Sometimes you must prepare your heart to sacrifice the promise, maybe reasons unknown to man.

Isaac was born with a purpose and Isaac was promised to Abraham and Sarah in their older age. Sarah was barren and could not produce any children and now at

98 years of age, although Sarah was way past childbearing age, here comes baby Isaac, the prophecy, the promised delivered right on time.

As Abraham would follow God's command, I could imagine Abraham took Isaac by the hand, leading him to Mount Moriah to be the sacrificed…I could imagine the pain Abraham must have felt and notice, nowhere does it mentioned that Abraham discussed this trip with Sarah and rightfully so, because Abraham knew that no way Sarah would allow her baby, her one and only son, Isaac to be sacrificed without putting up a fight.

I know what I'm talking about right here. I have a son and trust me I'm not easily parting with my son. Now if the Lord told me to part from my son, of course I would but I would agonize over it day and night and the Lord would be the only one who could bring such a healing and peace to my heart.

I love the conversation that Abraham and Isaac is having on their way to Mount Moriah. Isaac asked his daddy where is the sacrificial lamb, not knowing that he would be the sacrifice. Abraham, wise and strong in his faith, replied to Isaac, 'that God would provide the sacrificial lamb.'

> **Genesis 22:11-14** – *Abraham, Abraham, the angel of the Lord call out. Abraham replied, "Here I am." "Do not lay your hand on the boy or do anything to him, for now I know that you fear God, seeing you have not withheld your son, your only son, from me."*

God knew that above any and everything in the world, Abraham trusted and loved God more than anything. As verse 13 would have it – a ram was there and by verse 14 Abraham named that place Jehovah Jireh, which is translated to mean God provides.

Isn't it funny how God the Father asked Abraham to do something that one day He would do for us...offer up His ONLY begotten Son. Jesus did come and offer Himself as a sacrifice, just as the Bible said that He would. Because of His sacrifice, everyone will be saved from spiritual death by the Resurrection and all can be saved from their sins through faith in Jesus Christ. Christ's atoning sacrifice marked the end of sacrifices by the shedding of blood. (Hebrews 10).

JESUS BECAME THAT PERFECT SACRIFICE!

Although Abraham didn't have to follow all the way through physically, his faith had to follow through. Even when we don't understand the sacrifices that are required of us, just always remember the One who loves us and know that we may not always understand the "why" behind the scene of every scenario in our lives. If you can't trust man with the promise – trust God with the promise. God never allows us to experience loss and not make it back up to us.

Even today, God's people have always sacrificed greatly and in many ways. Some sufferings we may have to endure is never even spoken about. Some have suffered hardship and ridicule for the gospel. Sometimes you lost friends along the way. Some have even lost their jobs while others have lost their lives. Whatever the sacrifice(s) may be, the Lord notices our sacrifices and He has promised, *"Every one that hath forsaken houses, or brethren, or sisters, or father, or mother, or wife, or children, or lands, for my name's sake, shall receive an hundredfold, and shall inherit everlasting life"* (Matthew 19:29). Not just those that are in marriages, but those that have loved ones, children, and friends; we make sacrifices constantly because that's what love does.

We understand in the Bible when a sacrifice was made, it was made to cover sin and to bring atonement and peace to the people. Even then, God said He rather He had obedience than sacrifice. God already knows if we would just listen and trust Him as we should, we could prevent a lot of the heartaches; only if we would allow Him to lead us.

I know that God's ways are not always our ways and sometimes we do not understand God's ways but He tells us *not to lean on our own understanding but in our ways, acknowledge Him* (Proverbs 3:5). We see what's happening now but God knows what's going on behind the scenes and He knows what will happen in the future.

I understand now, in a marriage, you can be willing to put in the 100% and then some but if the other person is not willing, the marriage cannot survive. Sacrifices must be made on both people's part. Both parties have got to want the marriage to live. Your marriage can only be what you make it and yes, marriage is work but marriage is not just all work, marriage can be fun and marriage should be a lifelong partnership.

I love the relationship that I have with my husband. Not only do we love each other unconditionally, we work very well together because we work as a team. We understand that we're not working against each other but we are working with each other and for one another. We're a team and I'm so glad that we are a winning team! To God be ALL the glory!

IF SEASONS CHANGE - WHY NOT YOU?

Nothing remains the same. Ecclesiastes 3:1 tells us *to everything, there is a season, and a time to every purpose under the Heaven.*

I remember during President Obama's first presidential race, he used the word 'change' a lot. First, the President understood early on that it was necessary for the old way of doing things to change if he wanted to be a successful President and if he wanted the people to have a better a standard of living. You probably heard that phrase, "keep doing what you are doing and you will keep getting what you are getting." For something to change, you have to do things differently from what you are accustomed to doing.

The first place change has to occur is with how we think; our mindsets must change. Although we have to see things differently, we also have to do things differently. Whether welcomed or unwelcomed, change will come into our lives almost on a daily basis. My previous husband once said to me that I was trying to change him and that he didn't want to change. As a wife, I was really trying to help him because that's what wives do. My husband at that time wouldn't allow me to fulfill my role as a wife to him. Of course, I began to think about what he said, "you are trying to change me, and I don't want to change." This was one of the most disturbing statements that I had ever personally heard.

I recognized immediately from early on nothing remains the same, not even the leaves on the tree. We are all a work in progress and if we do not see the need to better ourselves, then we will be where we are forever and that, my friend, would be arrested development.

As previously mentioned, Solomon talked about change in Ecclesiastes 3. Then Solomon goes on to name many things that take place in these seasons of change but what I like is that with every season of change in our lives, there is purpose and there is a reason even for the unpleasant things that may come. Have you ever noticed that it seems like out of the worst situations, the best things end up being produced?

Even with myself, out of a bad marriage comes a book. Out of a bad marriage comes knowledge and experience. You can take a bad situation and help somebody else. In other words what could have been hurtful, embarrassing and a failure, God somehow turned that thing around and allowed you to continue to be compassionate, allowed you to be able to hold your head up and at the same time experience success and happiness. *All things work together for the good of them that love the Lord and is called according to his purpose* (Romans 8:28). Yes, as I mentioned before God has a purpose for each and every one of our lives. That's my prayer, that I fulfill the purpose for which I was put on this Earth.

As we continue on life's journey, we are going to have certain struggles that come into our lives but we have to be equipped to handle them. I'm not saying that we will never be afraid, angry, sad or just plain unhappy with certain events that might arise in our lives but we don't have to let that unpleasant state linger in our lives longer than they have to. The faster we recognize what's going on, the faster we can deal with it and allow God to bring us healing. Don't you want to be made whole?

I remember when I was a little girl, about five years old, my daddy and I were walking around the apartment building where we lived. The sun was shining, it was just a beautiful day and although I enjoyed that moment and I was filled with so much joy, something deep down inside knew that one day my daddy wouldn't be with me.

This knowing made my time with him that moment so much dearer to me. I don't know how I knew it. I don't know if it was the fact of Poppa Seal passing away on Christmas Eve or was it the fact that I knew that my dad was older (my daddy was 55 years of age when I was born). I truly thank God for those precious memories. My daddy made his transition in November of 1983 and I was 18 years old, away at college at the time. Then my mom would make her transition some 11 months later in October of 1994.

As we can see, nothing remains the same. Somehow you get through these difficult things that we all have to go through. Of course, I miss both my father and my mother but I know that they wouldn't want me to be stuck grieving for them for the rest of my life. Do I love my parents – Absolutely! Do I miss my parents – without question. Just as we know that nothing remains the same, we also know what King Solomon said in the Book of Ecclesiastes that there is a season for everything; there's a time to be born and a time to die.

I know for this very reason, even some people that come into our lives can and will be there only for a season. Instead of getting upset when friends began to pull away, just thank God for the times He allowed you to be with your friend and move on. People change every day and you too must change and move on.

I believe that there are a few reasons why people do not like to change. One reason is because that person hasn't recognized that they need to change, which again, I will label that as arrested development. Another reason why people do not like to change is because of fear. We get comfortable or complacent where we are or doing what we are accustomed to doing; keep doing what you are doing and you will keep getting what you are getting. We hear this phrase so much until it has become cliché but this phrase is so true. If what you are currently doing isn't working, then you clearly need to change that.

In some cases, in our mind, we already know that change needs to come but we don't know how to go through the process or we just don't want to go through the process. Yes, the process of changing can be difficult, painful amongst other things, but the quicker we make those changes, the better off we all will be.

YOU'VE GOT TO MOVE FOR THE BLESSING

> ***Genesis 12:1-2*** – *Now the LORD had said unto Abram, Get thee out of thy country, and from thy kindred, and from thy father's house, unto a land that I will shew thee: ² And I will make of thee a great nation, and I will bless thee, and make thy name great; and thou shalt be a blessing.*

What we need to understand here is that Abram, whose name would later change to Abraham, was already wealthy. Being that Abram was obedient and moved in the season when God told him to move, God made Abram even wealthier. Abram was also a blessing to other people. I don't know all the reasons of why God had Abram to move but I do realize that when we move in a timely manner according to God's plan, things will line up in our lives the way they're supposed to.

I believe that sometimes God moves you away from different people because sometimes He wants to do something for you at that time that does not concern others. Yes, I said it! Everything God has for you might not be for the people that you are currently hanging around and yes, some of those people can be your family and close friends.

We must remember where we were might have been good but where God wants to take us is even better. Just as Abram had to travel with his immediate family, his nephew Lot, his servants, and all of his cattle, I'm sure this was not an easy process but it was a necessary process. Sometimes we choose to stay where we are because of comfort but if we want to reap all of the blessings that the Lord has for us, not only is it necessary for us to move but it is necessary for us to move in the season that God tells us to move.

This move might not be a physical move. Sometimes it's necessary for us to move away from the way we think and other times it might be for us to move away from some of the things that we are doing. Wherever the change may need to take place, we need to learn to go with the flow so that we can grow or become what God want us to be and grow to where God wants us to be.

A lot of things that we go through in life are not just because we took a wrong path or chose the wrong thing to do; I really believe that the Lord will allow us to go through certain situations so that we can help others or, just like in Abram's case, be a blessing to others. If you never had a problem, how would you know that your God could solve them?

No matter how painful a situation is, you must move past thinking about how it brought you so much grief. Growth is painful. Change is painful. But nothing is as painful as staying stuck somewhere you don't belong. You might ask how does one move from the place of pain, grief, sorrow, hurt or bitterness? Remember, a broken and contrite heart God will not despise. God is near to those that grieve; all you have to do is pray and believe that God will heal your hurt. It doesn't matter if it's a dear friend that has chosen to walk out of your life; or if it's someone close who has made their transition or even if it's a marriage that has ended in divorce. Although you might be broken beyond anything you could have ever imagined or believed, do not allow your brokenness to run deeper than the belief that you have in God.

After you've decided that you can no longer stay in the place where you are, you need to allow God to heal the hurt. A lot of times when we try to deal with things on our own, we might end up turning to people and things that we should not turn to while this is the time we should just turn to the Lord.

Never allow your brokenness to take you to a place that you don't want to be or to a place that you don't need to be. It's okay to hurt, it's okay to grieve but it's not okay to self-destruct. Sometimes the pain that a person is feeling can reach a place so deep down inside of them and for some that hurt may seem so unbearable that they will turn to the wrong people for advice, they will turn to alcohol and/or drugs and yes, some have even committed suicide all because they did not know how to cope. I even believe that some people who have been on drugs for many years and finally overdosed on drugs really had a long, drawn out suicide. All I'm saying is that turn to God.

***Jeremiah 29:11** – For I know the thoughts that I think toward you, saith the LORD, thoughts of peace, and not of evil, to give you an expected end.*

God wants good things for all of us. Let's allow Him to give those things to us. God is not a respecter of person but He said in His Word that He is a rewarder of them that diligently seek Him.

Move on from that place of hurt and deceit that has been holding you captive and move into that place where God's blessings are overflowing and then teach other people to do the same.

THE ELEVENTH HOUR

As I thought that I had completed this book, the Lord told me to go back and talk about the eleventh hour. The eleventh hour came when I was getting my divorce. The courtroom that I was initially in had to go into another courtroom because our judge was not there that day. I watched many cases come before the judge, ten to be exact. Some people had attorneys with them and others like myself were Pro Se. Pro Se is a legal term which means to represent oneself in person, in court before a judge, as in the case of one who does not retain a lawyer and appears on the behalf of himself or herself in court.

I was the **11th** person to go before judge and when my case was called, I looked at the clock and the clock showed **11:00am**. I knew immediately that the Lord was speaking to me but I didn't know what He was saying at that time.

I approached the bench and I simply explained my case to judge; my version was short and to the point. The judge had me to repeat my statement to the court reporter.

After repeating my statement, the judge said that I was divorced as of that day and the judge signed off on my divorce at that very moment. I sat through ten other cases and all ten of those cases the judge simply said that the case would be reviewed and that the court would get back to them in two weeks. Again, I knew that something was different.

I was amazed but I knew that I was at the right place and the right time. When something happened "in the 11th hour", it means that it happened at the very last minute, at the last possible moment. It also has a positive association – it usually means that something good happened at the last possible moment. If you are familiar with the phrase "in the nick of time" it is very similar to saying "in the 11th hour". The original meaning of the 11th hour comes from the Bible, which at the time of the divorce, I did not know this. The eleventh hour which the Bible points us to is Matthew 6 chapter and you can find the eleventh hour mentioned twice in the sixth and ninth verse. In this context, that 11th hour meant it was around 5:00 p.m.; time was winding down for them. In traditional Jewish cultures, nothing was done after the evening hours.

I do thank the Lord because if I had not gone through that I would not be where I am today. I have a wonderful husband who loves and adores me and I him; not only do we love each other, we're friends, and we work well together. I need to pause right here, 'Thank you Lord!' Just don't want to take anything for granted.

I don't take what I've gone through for granted. Sometimes God will use what you've been through to help someone else. I could remember being at a dinner and I met this young lady for the very first time. The ladies were conversing and the men were enjoying one another. This young lady had just recently been divorced and I took her hands and I told her that I believed that she knew how to be a wife. Sometimes things happened that were beyond our control and just because it happened, it doesn't mean that you've done something wrong. The lady began to cry and tell me the story. I pray and believe that she's in a better a place today because that's just the kind of God we serve.

I left the courtroom feeling many different emotions at that time. I felt hurt of course but in a strange kind of a way I felt relieved and a sense of freedom. Remember, when I left that court room that day I still didn't know what the 11 represented; however, it would take me two long years for the Lord to finally reveal too me what the 11 meant. One day my son and I were watching this movie that he selected and thought was funny; it was supposed to have been a comedy. The lady in the movie was fake crying and said that "Johnny had saved her in the 11th hour. Immediately, I told my son to pause the TV and I began to explain what had happened in court that day.

I knew then that God had saved me from something; not sure what but anytime you need to be saved from something, it can't be good. That revelation helped me to move forward and close a chapter in my life so that I could move on. Not only did the Lord save me but He freed me to move on to the next phase of my life.

2 Corinthians 3:17 – *Where the spirit of the Lord is, there is liberty.*

He wants us to be free from all hurt, guilt, and shame. God really does want us to be free and He wants us to experience the peace that He talks about in the Bible.

A BROKEN ECONOMY BEING MADE WHOLE

Generally, I try to stay away from subjects like this but since we are talking about brokenness in today's time you cannot help but talk about the broken economy in which we live. Now, if I would have written this book back in 2007, although the economy needed repairing back then, I believe this would have been a topic that I could have overlooked.

Where do I start? Of course with the government. Just so that I'm not beating up on any president in particular, I'll just go on to say that whether democratic or republican, I believe that they are all a part of one party. Dr. James W. Wardner wrote in his book entitled <u>The Planned Destruction of America</u> that a recession is the result of monetary ignorance and that a depression is the result of monetary abuse. I'm not writing this to complain or transfer blame from one party to the next or to put blame on any one person. I'm writing this to tell the truth as I know it.

From the very beginning, the government could never carry itself. I don't care who's currently the president or whomever will be our next president; it is a known fact Biblically that the government cannot and will not be able to stand or remain. Let me shed some light here.

Isaiah 9:6 *– For unto us a child is born, unto us a son is given: and the government shall be upon His shoulder: and his name shall be called Wonderful, Counsellor, The mighty God, The everlasting Father, The Prince of Peace.*

This scripture is talking about Jesus. Long before Jesus even came to planet Earth, it was prophesied that, "the government shall be upon His shoulder." I saw two things here: 1) Anything that you have to carry on your shoulder cannot carry itself; 2) Anything that cannot carry itself and you have to carry it on your shoulder is a burden. Yes, the government is a burden that cannot carry itself.

Think of a new baby that you have to carry everywhere. Yes, that's what our government was back then and that's what our government is today, an immature baby that will never be able to walk on its own. Wow, some powerful truth right there.

> ***2 Peter 2:10*** *– But chiefly them that walk after the flesh in the lust of uncleanness, and despise government. Presumptuous are they, self-willed, they are not afraid to speak evil of dignities.*

We hear a lot of people complaining and talking about the government and rightfully so but when we get into name-calling and saying unethical things that is downright wrong and rude, I personally will never be a supporter of that. It's just down right disrespectful.

> ***Isaiah 9:7*** *– Of the increase of his government and peace there shall be no end, upon the throne of David, and upon his kingdom, to order it, and to establish it with*

judgment and with justice from henceforth even forever. The zeal of the LORD of hosts will perform this.

Yes, there will be a new government that Jesus will head up forever. There will be everlasting peace with justice in this government. Jesus will treat the people fairly, with love and respect.

Let me just shift gears for a second, the Book of Revelation the 6th chapter deals with judgment. The judgments that will come upon the Earth will be many and will come in the form of famine, wars, sickness, and even death.

> ***Revelation 6:5-6*** *– And when he had opened the third seal, I heard the third beast say, Come and see. And I beheld, and lo a black horse; and he that sat on him had a pair of balances in his hand. ⁶ And I heard a voice in the midst of the four beasts say, A measure of wheat for a penny, and three measures of barley for a penny; and see thou hurt not the oil and the wine.*

Although, the scripture states that wheat and three measures of barley was for a penny, this was like a whole day's wage and what John was clearly trying to point out here is that the food was overpriced and if you paying a full day's wage for food then that would cost a famine. Not only can a world not live that way but remember that is a great injustice to people as a whole and God is a God of justice.

So who is allowing these things to occur? The government is allowing these things to happen when companies are allowed to send work overseas so that they can receive these big tax breaks and downsize thousands of employees, causing them to be out of jobs thus leaving them with little or no money and healthcare. Look what John saw in Revelation 21: *And I saw a new Heaven and a new earth: for the first Heaven and the first earth were passed away; and there was no more sea. ² And I John saw the holy city, New Jerusalem, coming down from God out of Heaven, prepared as a bride adorned for her husband.*

I read in a newsletter many years ago about the Hubble Telescope being able to see a city coming closer to the Earth every year. I'm sure that I have that article packed somewhere; however, I read that the Hubble Space Telescope was put in space to take high quality pictures for us to study and learn from.

The Hubble Telescope was meant to launch in 1986 but the explosion of space shuttle Challenger delayed the launch until 1990. It is said that The Hubble Space Telescope is an un-manned orbiting observatory and that because of the Hubble Telescope, we now know how big and how old the universe is. It is said that the Hubble Telescope examined the composition of a world around another star. Could this be another city?

Could this be the city that John talks about in the Book of Revelation? "The New Jerusalem coming down from God out of Heaven?" I think that it's a great possibility that it is. Well, it doesn't matter how many trips is made in outer space, it doesn't matter how many 'high quality' pictures that are being taken by the Hubble Space Telescope and it doesn't matter how much money one has, if you do not accept Jesus as your personal Savior you will not be residing in that city.

Revelation 21:3-6 *– And I heard a great voice out of Heaven saying, Behold, the tabernacle of God is with men, and he will dwell with them, and they shall be his people, and God himself shall be with them, and be their God. 4 And God shall wipe away all tears from their eyes; and there shall be no more death, neither sorrow, nor crying, neither shall there be any more pain: for the former things are passed away. 5 And he that sat upon the throne said, Behold, I make all things new. And he said unto me, Write: for these words are true and faithful. 6 And he said unto me, It is done. I am Alpha and Omega, the beginning and the end. I will give unto him that is athirst of the fountain of the water of life freely.*

God said it, that settles it and it is so. There will be a new Heaven and a new earth. This period on earth will be what is referred to as the millennial. You will not find millennium in the Bible but you will find the thousand years that God refers to as that time that satan will be locked up for a thousand years. (Revelations 20:1-3).

Yes, satan will be released briefly to go to battle one last and FINAL time. I asked the LORD why would satan be released upon the earth again after he was locked up and what came into my spirit is that the tribulation period was supposed to be seven years but the LORD is going to cut the tribulation period short to about 5 ½ years because He said if He doesn't cut the tribulation period short there will be no mankind left. You know satan is a fool and his objective remains the same, he comes to kill, steal and destroy. Think about it…satan got kicked out of Heaven. He knows what Heaven is like and he knows that he will never have the option of going back to Heaven; misery does love company. he knows that he can never return to Heaven and that he's doomed so he wants to take as many people with him.

***Matthew 24:22** – And except those days should be shortened, there should no flesh be* *saved: but for the elect's sake those days shall be shortened.*

You know what else I believe? I believe that satan knows that hurts God when we allow satan to deceive us and when people here on planet earth don't accept Jesus as their personal Lord and Savior. I believe it hurts God because He gave us the Perfect Gift but many will refuse the Gift. The Gift of Salvation!

I believe that if the Christian today transitioned, go to sleep, or died today that we would be in Heaven with the Lord. I do believe during the thousand years (millennial) period that some saints will live on earth. I do not believe that the thousand years (millennial) is now but I do believe that it's soon to come.

After the millennial period, I do believe that some saints will have both access to the New Heaven and the New Earth, which will be the New Jerusalem. One reason why I believe that there will be a New Heaven and a New Earth (Jerusalem) is because God created a place or places where the devil has never been. Maybe, God did this as to be rid of sin once and for all! I believe that the New

Jerusalem or the New City that John saw coming down from Heaven was created because the antichrist is going to set himself up in the temple in Jerusalem and desecrate it. When the antichrist set himself up in temple like he is God, this will cause the temple to become defiled.

Write: for these words are true and faithful.

Revelation 21:1-7 *– And I saw a new Heaven and a new earth: for the first Heaven and the first earth were passed away; and there was no more sea. ² And I John saw the holy city, new Jerusalem, coming down from God out of Heaven, prepared as a bride adorned for her husband. ³ And I heard a great voice out of Heaven saying, Behold, the tabernacle of God is with men, and he will dwell with them, and they shall be his people, and God himself shall be with them, and be their God. ⁴ And God shall wipe away all tears from their eyes; and there shall be no more death, neither sorrow, nor crying, neither* *shall there be any more pain: for the former things are passed away. 5 And he that sat upon the throne said, Behold, I make all things new. And he said unto me, Write: for these words are true and faithful. 6 And he said unto me, It is done. I am Alpha and Omega, the beginning and the end. I will give unto him that is athirst of the fountain of the water of life freely. 7 He that overcometh shall inherit all things; and I will be his God, and he shall be my son.*

When you see the desolation of abomination in the temple, then you will know that we have entered the tribulation period. There is no temple in Jerusalem and have not been for over 2,000 years. Currently, there is great discussion surrounding the rebuilding of the temple.

https://www.breakingisrael**news**.com/tag/**rebuilding-the-third-temple**/

When you see the antichrist with the mark to his head and he dies and come back to life for all to see – then we would have been in the tribulation period for 3 ½ years already. I do believe that the saints of God will experience great persecution, even some unto death. I do believe as a whole the church is NOT prepared mentally or emotionally to endure such horrific things. I do PRAY that God makes us ready. I do believe that a rapture will take place in the earth where God will usher ALL of His people out of the earth; I just do not agree with the timing of when this will be done.

Some people think that God will rapture the Church out of the earth before the tribulation period. I firmly believe that it will be after the tribulation period. Who are the saints that had been beheaded and souls where crying out unto the Lord in the Book of Revelations 7^t?

> ***Revelation 7:9-10, 13-14** – After this I beheld, and, lo, a great multitude, which no man could number, of all nations, and kindreds, and people, and tongues, stood before the throne, and before the Lamb, clothed with white robes, and palms in their hands; [10] And cried with a loud voice,*

saying, Salvation to our God which sitteth upon the throne, and unto the Lamb. 13 And one of the elders answered, saying unto me, What are these which are arrayed in white robes? and whence came they? 14 And I said unto him, Sir, thou knowest. And he said to me, These are they which came out of great tribulation, and have washed their robes, and made them white in the blood of the Lamb.

I'm so glad that this story does not end right here.

Revelation 21:1-7 *– And I saw a new Heaven and a new earth: for the first Heaven and the first earth were passed away; and there was no more sea. 2 And I John saw the holy city, New Jerusalem, coming down from God out of Heaven, prepared as a bride adorned for her husband. 3 And I heard a great voice out of Heaven saying, Behold, the tabernacle of*

God is with men, and he will dwell with them, and they shall be his people, and God himself shall be with them, and be their God. 4 And God shall wipe away all tears from their eyes; and there shall be no more death, neither sorrow, nor crying, neither shall there be any more pain: for the former things are passed away. 5 And he that sat upon the throne said, Behold, I make all things new. And he said unto me, Write: for these words are true and faithful. 6 And he said unto me, It is done. I am Alpha and Omega, the beginning and the end. I will give unto him that is athirst of the fountain of the water of life freely. 7 He that overcometh shall inherit all things; and I will be his God, and he shall be my son.

This is why Christians PRAY, this is why Christians go faithfully to the CHURCH, this is why Christians are PERSECUTED today. This is why Christians are STRONG.

This is why Christians do not GIVE UP. There's something bigger and greater that is happening in the earth right now! Just as the Apostle Paul commissioned Timothy to be strong, I believe that the LORD has commissioned us to be strong today. We were created for such a time as this! Therefore, Christians are the LIGHT of WORLD.

If you're reading this book right now and you've made it to the end of this book; I BELIEVE that you have been CHOSEN for such a time as this. I believe you will now begin to understand all of the pitfalls, obstacles and hard trials that you have had endured. I believe if you've made it this far, there is nothing else to do but to fulfill your God given purpose in the earth.

It's your time to RISE up! My PRAYER for you right now is to take your rightful place in the earth! Everything that you've been through brought you to this place for SUCH A TIME AS THIS! My PRAYER is that God will continue to enlighten you, continue to strengthen you and continue to direct your path! You've come too far to turn around now.

Broken Beyond Belief

No matter what's going on in your life in you or around you - my advice to you today is 'STAY FOCUSED.' I read the end of the BOOK (the Bible) and we WIN!

ABOUT THE AUTHOR

Vida Buckley grew up on the West side of Chicago, Illinois with her father and mother and her three siblings. Later, her father and mother would separate but decided to remain married until death did they part.

Vida is an Evangelist, Writer, Speaker and Seminar Orator. She accepted the call into the ministry March 1997 and was licensed as a minister by Pastor Carolyn Jenkins, Oakton Community Church, Evanston, Illinois.

After preaching her very first sermon "Help Is on the Way," the church was led into a congregational song "I'm on the Battle Field for the Lord!" And that has been her constant testimony throughout the years. Through many ups and downs, Vida remains faithful to God and she remains on the battlefield for the Lord!

Vida would later be ordained as an evangelist by Bishop Dexter Thompson and Apostle Helen McCullough, High Praise Ministries, Chicago, Illinois.

Currently, Vida Buckley attends True Faith P.B. Church, Chicago, Illinois under Pastor James O. Hampton where she teaches Sunday School and minister regularly alongside her husband Elder Gerald Buckley.

Broken Beyond Belief

www.ingramcontent.com/pod-product-compliance
Lightning Source LLC
LaVergne TN
LVHW052254070426
835507LV00035B/2563